Business Analysis: The Question and Answer Book

SANDHYA JANE

Copyright © 2018 Sandhya Jane
All rights reserved.
ISBN-13: 97809906374-4-8

This book is strictly meant for the reader's personal consumption only. It is an academic as well as professional book and meant for such reference. This book shall NOT be re-produced, re-sold or given away to other people. If you would like to share this book with another person, please ask them to attend the training to obtain an official copy. If you're reading this without buying the book or it was not obtained through official means, then please return or write to the author (sandhya@sandhyajane.com or Sandhya.jane@gmail.com) or publisher (info@anisans.com), to obtain an official copy. Thank you for respecting the hard work of author and the investment made by an institute to produce this work.

Since, this is a first draft created for test purposes, it will be periodically enhanced and enriched in terms of quality, presentation, citation and more over time.

Permission is required to re-use or distribute this book.

To,
Team ANISAN:
Staff, students, and supporters

CONTENTS

BUSINESS ANALYSIS: THE QUESTION AND ANSWER BOOK I
PREFACE I
FOREWORD IV

1 INTRODUCTION 7
    1.1 BUSINESS ANALYSIS 8
    1.2 THE BUSINESS ANALYST'S ROLE 14

2. IDEAS AND STRATEGY 46
    2.1 STRATEGY ANALYSIS 47
    2.2 BUSINESS NEED 50
    2.3 STAKEHOLDER ANALYSIS 61
    2.4 GAP ANALYSIS 72
    2.5 BUSINESS CASE 81
    2.6 SOLUTION SCOPE 86
    2.7 STRATEGY ANALYSIS TECHNIQUES 109

3 PROJECT MANAGEMENT 121
    3.1 SOFTWARE DEVELOPMENT LIFE CYCLE 122
    3.2 APPROACHES 129
    3.3 AGILE 133

4 REQUIREMENT MANAGEMENT LIFE CYCLE 145
    4.1 ELICITATION PLANNING 152
    4.2 ELICITATION PROCESS 158
    4.3 REQUIREMENT MANAGEMENT 172
    4.4 CHANGE MANAGEMENT: 202
    4.5 REQUIREMENT ELICITATION TECHNIQUES 216

5 REQUIREMENT VERIFICATION AND VALIDATION 226
    5.1 REQUIREMENT QUALITIES 227

6 UNIFIED MODELLING LANGUAGE 234

- 6.1 UML 235
- 6.2 USE CASE 238
- 6.3 DATA MODELLING 257
- 6.4 ACTIVITY DIAGRAM/PROCESS DIAGRAM 261
- 6.5 STATE DIAGRAM 269

7 DISPOSITION 274

8 ESSENTIALS OF BUSINESS ANALYSIS 278
- 8.1 TYPES OF TESTING 279
- 8.2 SAMPLE TEST CASE 296
- 8.3 USER ACCEPTANCE TESTING 298

9 REFERENCE DIAGRAMS 299

10 REFERENCE 302

11 AKNOWLEDGEMENT 312

Preface

Simplicity is the ultimate Sophistication

- Steve Jobs

Based on this statement by one of my favorite entrepreneurs, I have decided to decode business analysis in the simplest format possible without being simplistic. Also, I intend to simplify the world of business analysis to help you gain the confidence in your career.

The primary goal of this book is to present business analysis in a format that can clearly be understood by both technical and non-technical professionals. It can even be referred to by small business or process owners who intend to improve their business or operational processes with the help of information technology. These stakeholders can refer this work to improve the productivity of their teams through implementation of efficient processes and systems.

This book will also be useful in providing detailed insights to students or professionals who are keen on business analysis as a career.

In this book I seek to comprehensively cover principles and practices such as theory, illustrations, case studies, and practical applications.

Therefore, a conscious attempt has been made to make the book as comprehensive as possible so that it can be used in most situations. However, the business analyst may use it wherever it is relevant or modify it whenever it is so required. At the end of a day, it is not so much about the right or wrong approaches to a problem but defining the most relevant solution. Since one size does not fit all, one template or one process or business analysis procedure may not fit everyone. You, as the reader, can therefore construct your solution based on this eternal truth.

As in any other profession, a would-be business analyst has to go through the rigors of the interview process in order to prove his knowledge, skill, competency, and worth to a prospective employer. The business analysis professionals are also required to obtain certification from an accredited institution to deepen their knowledge and understanding of the domain, and validate the same to the prospective recruiters.

The further intent of this book is to offer a comprehensive guide to help business analysts to prepare for a role. The Q&A format of the book guides the reader in planning and organizing their thoughts in a focused and structured manner.

In addition, the aim of this book is to not only clarify existing concepts but also help professionals enhance their knowledge base by introducing them to new concepts, which is likely to come in handy in their professional lives later.

Thus, the book can also be used for preparing for professional certification exams offered by several leading institutes across the globe.

It has been my conscious endeavor to make this work an in-depth source of knowledge for IT and management students. In the process, the book may also guide an interviewer to conduct interviews effectively.

I have attempted to write this book from my own professional experiences in the corporate and academic world, including teaching and mentoring would-be business analysts. I have also tried to present the invaluable feedback shared by my students of practices and procedures adopted in diversified industries globally.

Several answers provided in the book have been written and reviewed by other senior business analysis professionals in the industry. It is, therefore, my hope that the work will be of immense value to not only beginners but also established professionals.

Having said that, the reader must understand an interview question and its context before attempting it, as some questions may require a bespoke answer. The reader is, therefore, advised to use answers provided here as the base to prepare his own customized responses. Adding real life experiences, while elaborating a point, is highly recommended.

- Sandhya Jane

Foreword

Data is the new oil – it is the asset upon which a country's or corporation's success depends upon in what has been termed as the age of the Fourth Industrial Revolution. Data science and analytics today are transforming industries, schools, hospitals, governments and societies in general. To support this transformation, millions of experts specializing in deriving knowledge from data will be required in the coming years.

A large part of innovation in technology during the late 20th century focused on the information technology infrastructure - storage capacity, the speed of data access and computing speed. However, technologies such as cloud computing and the in-memory storage of data for real-time access have now made information technology infrastructure an essential utility.

Consequently, the next set of innovations will focus on making intelligent use of the data for improving lives and transforming businesses. Though the concept of analytics has existed ever since the beginning of human civilization, the new tools that work with a much larger size of a disparate set of data make analytics the most important subject in today's world.

This book is an essential guidebook for practitioners of data analytics. It covers everything needed to work as a data scientist, business analyst, programmer, or CIO. In addition, project managers and engagement managers who work with customers in developing business insight solutions will also find this an indispensable reference.

While there are dozens of books on this topic, the unique format of questions and answers accelerates the learning process by mimicking an interactive discussion with a teacher. Those appearing for job interviews will especially find their key questions answered in this book. Therefore, I believe that this book will play an invaluable role in helping an aspiring business analyst not only in understanding the subject but also effectively participating in the job selection process.

Jobs in information technology are now moving away from infrastructure and application management to data management and analysis. Today, data scientists and business analysts are some of the highest paid jobs in the information industry. Going forward, a number of these jobs will likely clock double-digit growth over the next one decade.

During my days at IBM and SAP, I have witnessed the IT industry significantly transforming over the last ten years. Now most IT businesses are centered around the value IT brings to businesses. As a result, the role of IT is changing from a cost center to a revenue center, where businesses count on insights derived from data to drive sales, improve customer satisfaction, identify customer segments, develop offerings, and reduce costs.

Sandhya Jane is not only a teacher of the subject, she is also a practitioner and a business leader. These experiences provide her with a unique 360-degrees perspective of the subject and help her in developing the building blocks. Topics covered in the book connect business strategy, business processes, and operations management to technology, and develop the key concepts of data science, data modelling, and driving business results using data.

This is a breakthrough book. I hope you enjoy it and learn from it as much as I did.

Amitabh Satyam,
Former Managing Partner – SAP

1 Introduction

Business analysis is not a job; it is a profession. A person who does not feel passionate about this role will not excel.

— *Barbara A. Carkenord*

1.1 Business Analysis

Business: A business is also known as an enterprise, a company, or a firm, an entity that either produces goods or offers services either for profit or not-for-profit. For example, a manufacturing company offers a product and/or services to the customers. A car company produces cars and also manages service stations for servicing cars or selling their spare parts.

Similarly, a service company such as a hotel or hospital or courier company offers services for a certain charge, while a government entity offers services with or without charges. For example, a government official issues a birth certificate after verifying a newborn's birth details and receipt of the charges for processing the certificate. However, in most cases, state government provides free police service to keep cities safe.

A non-governmental organization (NGO) or a government department may offer their services such as free educational services to poor children. (The taxpayers may not be considered it as "free" services.)

The products or services are dependent on their market segment, services, and companies' policies. For example, five-star hotels and bed-and-breakfast motels offer services at different costs. There is a significant difference in the cost because of their market segment, customers' backgrounds and needs, and the overall quality of services.

Analysis: It means simply breaking down the information of an object, entity, process, or anything else to understand its functioning.

The information can be broken down in a various ways and followings questions depict some of the dimensions:

- What are components?
- How are they connected?
- What is the role of each component?
- How does each component function independently?
- How do these components function together?

To understand this, we simply break down the information in a systematic manner. For this, we can use a "functional decomposition", one of the business analysis techniques.

Let us use this technique to understand the admission process. ANISAN is a consulting and training firm. It provides training services to its customers and every participant who wishes to join the training is required to complete the admission process. How this admission process can be broken down systematically is shown in the picture below.

Process		ANISAN admission process				
Activity	1	Enquiry	2	Enrollment	3	Training
Task	1.1	Read course details online.	2.1	Create a login.	3.1	Receive the training material.
Task	1.2	Send the enquiry.	2.2	Make enrollment payment.	3.2	Receive the training link/address and details.
Task	1.3	Receive additional training detail, if required.	2.3	Receive the receipt for enrollment.	3.3	Attend the training.
Task	1.4	Send the queries, if any.	2.4	Read and Accept Training guideline.	3.4	Submit assignment.
Task	1.5	Receive the replies to the queries.	2.5	Fill out an admission form.	3.5	Complete online exam.
Task			2.6	Pay the training fees.	3.6	Collect the certificate.
Task			2.7	Receive the receipt for fees.		

In the above table, the admission function/process is broken down into three processes – enquiry, enrollment, and training. Subsequently, each process is further broken down into tasks. These tasks are indexed in a unique way to identify them easily.

If you wish to analyze an organization, you could consider one or more of the following points as necessary:
- Organization structure (What are business units? How are they connected? How do they communicate with each other?)
- Organization structure (What is the organization structure? What is the communication channel with the corporate office?)
- Customers/vendors/clients (Who are the customers or clients and what are their expectations?)
- Products/services/both (What are the products or services an organization offers?)
- Operations (How are these products/services delivered to the end customers/clients?)
- Business Processes (What are the main business processes?)
- Industry Regulations (What are the industry-specific regulations that are mandatory for an organization to comply?)
- Policies (What policies are applicable and how they are applicable, and what policies are not applicable?)
- Culture (How does the organization function? What are its core beliefs?)
- Technology (What are the major technologies utilized in supporting operations?)

To understand an organization and compare it with external entities or competitors, we need to consider the following points:
- Market Analysis (Analyzing the market trends on various parameters such as product, features, cost, customers, etc.)
- Current Trends (Analyzing the current trends using certain criteria such as growth, direction, product, features, etc.)
- Future Trends (Predicting future trends based on the past and current trends, and their growth history)
- Benchmarks (Comparing the products or services or other criteria with similar ones in the market)

1. What is a Business Change?

It is a change to achieve business goals to improve processes, technologies, and productivity. There are various reasons for business changes. They could be due to changes in product or services, organizational goals, technology enhancement, new requirements, new regulations or new business needs. (Please refer to the question on business need for more details.)

These business changes typically imply technology implementation, mergers & acquisitions, business process re-engineering, etc. Business change impacts the business, people, and technologies partially or completely, depending on the nature of the business change. Implementing business change requires a cohesive effort.

This term may be known as business change, business transformation, or simply changes. To avoid confusion and conflict between business change and requirement change, both these terms are explicitly mentioned throughout the book as either business change or requirement change.

The major difference between business change and business transformation is - while business change is applied to small or big business changes, initiatives or projects, business transformation is applied to only big changes.

Although this book primarily focuses on business change from a business and technology perspective, we have made an attempt to include a few aspects of other factors as well.

(Please refer to the 'business case' question for measuring the success of the business change.)

2. What is Business Analysis?

As per the International Institute of Business Analysis (IIBA), A Guide to the Business Analysis Body of Knowledge (BABOK), version 2.0,

"Business Analysis is a set of tasks and techniques to understand business needs (problems or opportunities) by analyzing the organization structure, culture, policies, and operations to recommending of the solution to the stakeholder of an organization in order to help it achieve its goals."

As per the IIBA's, BABOK Guide version 3.0, "Business analysis is the practice of enabling change in an enterprise by defining needs and recommending solutions that deliver value to stakeholders. Business analysis enables an enterprise to articulate needs and the rationale for change, and to design and describe solutions that can deliver value."

In addition to the above-mentioned factors, to analyze the current-state, the business analyst will have to study the products, services, operations (how products/services are delivered to the customer, how policies, and regulations, including internal and external regulations, affect the operations, etc.) and business needs. While recommending a solution, the business analyst will have to synthesize the market data before defining future-state. This ensures that the potential solution is suitable for current and future needs.

As mentioned in the "business analysis" book published by the British Computer Society (BCS), "Business Analysis as a practice helps facilitate change in an organization by defining business needs (problems or opportunities) in collaboration with its stakeholders through strategy analysis and requirement engineering (planning, elicitation, analysis, management, and validation). The recommended solution could be an IT or non-IT, minor or humongous and customized or off-the-shelf product."

3. What is the importance of a Business Analyst in an organization?

The business analyst plays a significant role in an organization by examining business needs and recommending solutions or improvements that are directly related to revenue, business risk, brand image, customer service, and/or business operations.

Also, the business analyst acts as a bridge between business stakeholders and IT stakeholders (IT team) by communicating and collaborating with business stakeholders and the technical team for defining and deploying the solution. This communication bridge is primarily to understand and communicate effectively with stakeholders from diversified backgrounds for understanding and accepting the collective vision of solution.

The business analyst also helps create an environment of transparency, openness and trust among team members to build a common platform to share ideas, and understanding of business change that eventually helps in mitigating the project risks.

The business analyst significantly contributes to the requirement management processes, including the requirement documentations for business and technical stakeholders to share the common project vision. These documents are created in standard templates and supported by models such as Unified Modelling Language (UML), process diagrams, Entity Relationship Diagrams (E-R Diagram), etc. These documentations serve as a basis for defining, designing, developing, testing, and deploying activities of the solution. Afterwards, they serve as the basis for a user manual.

4. What is Impact Analysis in business analysis field?

Impact analysis assesses the impact of the change (business or solution or requirement) on the business or solution. Depending on the nature of the change, it may have a limited impact on a particular business unit(s) or on the original requirement or on the entire organization. Impact analysis is conducted while defining the business needs, solution scope, requirement traceability, change management, and post-implementation.

1.2 The Business Analyst's Role

5. What is the Scope of business analyst role?

The scope of a business analyst's role can be broadly categorized into three main areas:
- Strategy Analysis
- Business Analysis
- IT System Analysis

[Paul, Yeats et al. 2011]

The following is a partial list of the scope within the lifecycle that covers all the areas mentioned above.

Business Strategy Analysis - Part I:

Such business analysts come from a business/domain background to define the business need, high-level solution scope, and present the business case to the sponsors.
- Business technology optimization and management
- Process management
- Define business need (problem or an opportunity)
- Define solution scope that would cater to that particular business need
- Define and present business case (cost vs. benefits analysis)
- Secure funding

Business Analysis:

These business analysts come from either business or technical backgrounds and start the core business analysis or requirement engineering once the business need is defined or project funding is arranged. These business analysts are primarily involved in eliciting requirements and defining solutions. Besides, they are also involved in identifying the IT team (internal or external) and managing it during solution development and implementation.

- Elicit requirements, document them, confirm them, scope them, present them, and get them approved or signed-off.
- Define solution or BRD or product roadmap
- Further requirement analysis (FRD, requirement models, etc.)
- Identify or recommend IT team (internal or external)
- Finalize solution and its scope

Business Strategy Analysis - Part II

- Verify and validate the solution against the enterprise need, current ability, and new business case analysis (cost vs. benefit) to accept the solution.

IT Business System or System Analysis:

These business analysts come from technical backgrounds and may possess software coding or testing skills. They primarily collaborate with members of the technical team to communicate requirements. They ensure that the software solution meets the requirements specified in the business solution. They also act as a bridge in translating and transferring business requirements into solution requirements (functional, non-functional, and technical constraints) to help the technical team understand business requirements correctly. In addition, IT business analysts also collaborate with implementation subject matter experts (SME) or production manager to elicit the transition requirements that are needed for moving the software solution into the user community.

- Support technical team in requirement and change management
- Oversee the development and testing activities
- Ensure implementation of high-quality solutions
- Close out documentations
- End-user training
- Enrich and enhance the solution during its lifecycle
- Ensure orderly termination of solution when it reaches the end of its lifecycle

Business Strategy Analysis - Part III

- ROI to review the business case (cost vs. benefits)
- Lessons learned

Data Business Analyst: The business analyst engaged in decision support systems works closely with business stakeholders to understand their roles and needs in terms of reports needed for effective decision-making. They also work with the market research team in projecting trends in the past, present, and future. In addition to business analysis skills, they are required to be well versed in SQL, data warehousing or other tools, and advanced MS-Excel and MS-Access to analyze data.

These are business analysts who deal with big data and statistics. They tend to crunch the numbers using algorithms and data models. In this sense, their role is similar to that of a data scientist. They tend to indicate the market trends for presenting them to stakeholders to facilitate the decision-making process.

Apart from the above, there may be specialized designations assigned to a business analyst, such as business process analyst (who is focused on process engineering) or product business analyst (who is involved in software product development), depending on their role.

6. **Can the business analyst's role be aligned with the software life cycle?**

SDLC Phase	Business Analyst Role
Initiation (Business Need Definition)	A business Need (opportunity or problem): • Defining the opportunity or a problem in details

Solution Scope / System concept Definition	Solution Scope: • Identifying scope of the solution in terms of features and functionalities. • Identifying the capacity in terms of performance, reliability, availability, scalability, environment, and operational needs. • Feasibility, initial risk analysis
Business Case (ROI or cost vs. benefit analysis)	Cost vs. Benefit: • Appropriateness studies for viability, and suitability • Business case - Feasibility and profitability of solution.
Project Planning	Business Analysis Planning • Requirement Planning (Plan for BA approach, Identify Stakeholders, Plan for BA governance, Plan for Information Management, Plan for BA performance)
Requirement Elicitation	Requirement Life Cycle • Eliciting (Gathering), Communicating, confirming, Analyzing, scoping, and documenting. • Defining solution • Preparing BRD (Business Requirement Documents) • Verifying and Validating the solution against organization need, strategy, capability and capacity i.e. appropriateness

Analysis and Designing	- Analyzing Requirements and preparing solution requirements - Designing through defining functional requirements, Non-Functional Requirement, (FRD – Functional Requirement Document) - Supporting the requirement description through Prototyping, modeling (UML) & Requirements verifications & validation (Design Catalogue) - Supporting Technical team in solution design, development and testing activities
Development	Development Phase Activities - Monitoring technical work to ensure the development is happening as per Functional requirements, - Reviewing and signing off the Test scenarios/test cases, - Preparing user manual, and completion of USE CASES. - Managing the changes to the requirements or solution.
Testing	Monitoring testing activities - Participating actively in daily testing-development team review meeting - Resolving issues, if any. - Conducting the user training. - Conducting the user acceptance testing.

Implementation	Roll out of the idea or request, • Monitoring the solution performance in production environment • Managing issues and problems during implementation. • Providing the status reports to the business stakeholders. • Conducting the user training.
Close out	o Submitting the post implementation documentation o Conducting the post implementation review
Operations and Maintenance	o Enriching and enhancing the solution by adding or removing features and functionalities (mini-projects) that are needed by the organization and stakeholders o Continuing the process as long as the solution is in its lifecycle
Decommissioning	o Planning for decommissioning o Informing relevant stakeholders about the last day of operation and future actions o Creating a list of data for archival: List of the data to be archived and the details of access right. o Planning and archiving the data after the last day of operations o Monitoring the technical team who archives the data as per the archival requirements o Monitoring technical team who disconnects, formats, and assigns the resources to other projects.

7. Who is Business Analyst?

A business analyst is a professional who is involved in any of the activities mentioned under the purview of business analysis.

As mentioned in the previous question, the role of a business analyst is primarily branched into strategy analysis, requirement engineering, and IT analysis. More details are mentioned below.

"Once charged mainly with defining and communicating requirements, business analysts (BAs) are increasingly expected to contribute everything from decision support, and return-on-investment (ROI) measures to new product development ideas. This high profile within organizations and across industries is in part attributable to its organizational role changing from an often-costly requirement to a potentially huge bottom-line booster. It's also fueled by a growing knowledge of how to better build and maintain the bridge between the IT and business worlds. While requirements remain the focus, business analysts are now expanding into all stages of solution design, development, and implementation." [Schreiner, 2007]

A business analyst can also be defined as: strategy analyst, stakeholder (one who is involved in strategy analysis), requirement engineer, project manager-business analyst (PM-BA), business analyst-quality analyst (BA-QA), product owner, product manager, consultant, management consultant, business system analyst, system analyst, UAT analyst, business analyst lead/manager (managing a business analysis team), change manager, IT analyst, etc., depending on their role and responsibilities within the organization.

8. What skill sets is a professional expected to possess when applying for a first business analyst position?

Check out the following business analysis competencies to review what tools or skills you need to focus on.

Behavioral and Personal Attributes: Communication, relationship building, influencing, team work, political awareness, analytical skills, critical thinking, attention to detail, problem-solving, self-confidence, and leadership qualities.

Business Knowledge: Domain knowledge, subject matter expertise, finance and economy, business case (cost vs. benefit analysis) development, vendor management, and organizational modelling.

Business Analysis Techniques: Project management, strategy analysis, stakeholder analysis and management, elicitation techniques, UML, process modelling, etc.

Additionally, the business analyst may also need to acquire project-specific knowledge and skills. For example, if the project requires them to work on a tool such as a business object or new domain such as new regulation, they will have to acquire the same.

The scope of business analysis is infinite, as it broadly deals with "improving business with or without the help of technology." Any work within that spectrum is business analysis. For example, this could apply to improving a small process within a department or implementing a regulatory framework across the industry or building a product. Apple had an app for music but couldn't use it independently. On the other hand, Hitachi developed a mini storage that could hold 1 GB of data, yet they didn't know what to do with it. Steve Jobs integrated both inventions to create iPod, which is one of the most commercially successful gizmos of our times.

It is important to obtain formal training and acquire the required knowledge and skill as well as PDUs to obtain professional certificate in business analysis, i.e., having official endorsements of one's knowledge and skills.

9. What does a successful business analyst do?

A successful business analyst adds value to the "business" through managing "business change", i.e., better business practices (Strategy Analysis) and better business technology management for an organization to enable them to achieve their goals. They provide solutions to support the launch of a new product/service or improve the production/delivery of the existing products/services and better customer service (i.e., operations).

To achieve that, the business analyst will put in additional effort in acquiring in-depth domain knowledge to understand stakeholders' requirements, complexities, business rules and related intricacies. The business analyst will use relevant domain language while collaborating with stakeholders and technical terms to collaborate with a technical team.

The business analyst will use tact in eliciting sensitive and challenging requirements. He needs to have an insight into the organizational dynamics and relationship among stakeholders.

The business analyst will understand business analysis deliverables and deliver them on time with an acceptable quality.

The business analyst will define the user requirements and minimum acceptance or quality criteria for each of them to ensure the solution meets end-user needs.

The business analyst must be reliable, sensitive and self-assured to collaborate with stakeholders effectively.

To simplify it further, the business analyst defines business, stakeholder, solution and transition requirements to define, develop, and deploy the solution or handle the business change.

Business Requirements: These are high-level requirements associated with the organizational goal. These are well-defined and well-structured requirements that define the solution to achieve business goals.

Stakeholder Requirements: Stakeholders will have their needs or requirements to interact with the solution based on their profile (role, responsibilities, and authority level). For example, a compliance subject matter expert (SME) will ensure that the new or improved processes are in-line with the internal and external compliance requirements. Or the customer service head will define requirements based on the organization's policies and process related to the customer services.

Solution Requirements: What capacity and condition a solution must have to achieve the above (business + stakeholder) requirements. They are specified as functional and non-functional requirements. In addition, the business analyst also defines business and technical constraints.

Transition Requirement: The additional requirements needed for the solution for transitioning it into the user community.

Business analysts drive the business change throughout the entire life cycle of a project by collaborating and communicating with the business and technical stakeholders.

They will assist in business adoption/change management activities and analyze/report on the impact of introduced solutions on the business. [BABOK v2 2008] [BABOK V3 2015] [Pohl and Rupp, 2011]

10. Can a business analyst drive the entire project? (This is for the PMBA role)

Yes, he can. Although the role of a business analyst is not very different from that of a project manager, the former also needs to add additional project management responsibilities to his existing briefs such as resource management, scheduling, budgeting, risk management and status reports management.

Delegating work to team members and monitoring the same closely are among his additional responsibilities. This involves activities such as development, testing, and implementation to ensure that the solution is in-line with requirements (FRD or SRS) and up to project management standards. In addition, the business analyst may solicit support from members of the technical team to learn some of the project-management-related activities. He can also learn through project documents, if available.

A business analyst on the IT side may report to the project manager or business analysis manager (or business analyst manager). However, this may be reversed if the business analyst on the business side is monitoring the IT vendor (service provider) team and overall project delivery.

11. What are the Business Analyst Artifacts (deliverables)?
The following is a list of major business analyst artifacts on the business and IT side. The artifacts or deliverables are dependent on the project approach, organizational standards, stakeholder comfort, and role of the Business Analyst.
- Business Need Document
- As-Is (Current State)
- To-Be (Future State)
- Gap Analysis
- Feasibility Study
- Solution Scope
- Business Case (Cost vs. Benefit Analysis)
- Return on Investment (ROI)
- Process or Activity Diagrams
- Enterprise Architecture, Organizational Modelling or Structure

- List of stakeholders as well as their roles, responsibilities, and description
- Activity List
- Work-breakdown structure for business analysis team
- Communication Plan
- Requirement repository planning details
- Requirement Traceability Matrix Document (RTM)
- Change Management Policy for the project (that includes roles and responsibilities of stakeholders involved in the change management process)
- Key performance areas for business analysis
- Requirement elicitation planning document
- Elicitation and Requirements
- List of stakeholder concerns
- Requirement and Scope Management documents
- List of approved requirements
- Business Requirement Documents (BRD) or Product Roadmap
- List of prioritized requirements
- Functional and Non-Functional Requirement Documents (FRD/NFRD) or Software Requirement Specifications (SRS)
- Use case catalogue
- State diagrams
- Data Modelling Diagrams (E-R diagrams or Class Diagrams)
- Data mapping
- Data dictionary
- Requirement verification checklist
- Testing reports
- User Acceptance Testing (UAT) review report
- Issue list
- Status list
- Additional modelling if required and done
- Result of other business analysis techniques during projects (such as functional decomposition diagram, dependency diagram, etc.)

- There are many other business analysis artifacts/deliverables that can be based on project need and organizational process assets/standards.

12. What are the main responsibilities of a business analyst?

The business analyst has a 360-degree role in the project, extending from the business to technology (IT) side.

On a business side, the business analyst is responsible for:

Strategy Analysis:
- Communicating and collaborating with stakeholders to achieve project and organizational goals
- Defining business need, i.e., problems or opportunities
- Defining solution scope with the help of project manager
- Feasibility study
- Defining business case (cost vs. benefit analysis or Return on Investment (ROI) before the project gets initial go or no-go

Requirement Management:
- Planning, elicitation, confirmation, organization, modelling, and documentation requirements
- Scoping, prioritization, categorization, and management of requirements
- Recommending of a solution
- Communicating and coordinating with business and technology teams throughout the solution (project) life cycle for a change management, issues, status and more.
- Clarifying any concerns and doubts, and providing supporting data/information, as necessary.

Additional Responsibilities
- Monitoring testing efforts

- Conducting or monitoring User Acceptance Testing (UAT) to gain acceptance, and ensuring the solution meets user expectations
- Supporting and monitoring implementation
- Guiding the business analysis team
- Supporting business stakeholders to become familiar with the new solution
- Creating a conducive environment on business and technology sides
- Ensuring delivery of high-quality solutions.
- Imparting user training whenever required
- Post-implementation documentation
- Archiving documents for future reference

13. What are the Knowledge Areas a business analyst need to know?

The business analyst needs to have the knowledge of business analysis, product management and technical know-how, including an understanding of testing.

Behavioral and personality related
- Analytical and cortical thinking skills
- Communication
- Relationship building
- Influencing and leadership skills
- Team player and team management skills
- Political awareness/understanding of organizational dynamics.
- Eye for detail
- Self-confidence to be able to convince others using hard data and factual information.

Business or Domain Knowledge
- Domain knowledge (product/services, operations and industry standards and industry regulations)
- Organization (products/services, customers, operations, policies, culture, organizational units, communication channels, key people)

- Stakeholders (project initiators, SMEs, users - internal and external, including customers/supplier)
- Strategy Analysis (to define business needs, solution scope, building business case, preparing Return On Investment (ROI)).
- IT environment (sophistication, adaptability, vision for IT) within the organization

IT Knowledge
- Business Change Management
- Project Management
- Requirement Engineering
- System Analysis
- Strategy Analysis *
- Data Mapping
- Data Dictionary
- Basics of Database (Basic SQL, Data Mapping, Data Dictionary) to communicate requirements
- Data Modelling
- Test Case/Test Scenario

Strategy Analysis *
- Impact Analysis
- Investigative Techniques
- Facilitation Techniques
- Business Technology Optimization
- Catwoe
- Consensus Modelling
- Force Field Analysis
- Six Thinking Hats
- SWOT Analysis
- Root Cause Analysis
- Competency Assessment
- Estimation
- Role Change
- Business Model Canvas

- Decision Modelling
- Functional Decomposition
- Business Change
- Business Capability Analysis
- Current State and Capability (As-Is)
- Future State and Ability (To-Be)
- Gap Analysis (To-Be – As-Is)
- Benchmarking and Market Analysis
- Financial Analysis /Business Case
- Defining solution and its scope
- Scope Modelling
- Organizational Structure and Modelling
- Stakeholder List, Map or Roles and Responsibilities
- Communication Policy and Standards
- Roles and Permissions
- Interview
- Workshop
- Business Process Modelling
- Concept Modelling
- Brainstorming
- Business Rules Analysis
- Document Analysis
- Interface Analysis
- Risk Analysis and Management
- Focus Groups
- Functional Decomposition
- Mind Mapping
- Observation
- User Stories
- Glossary
- Prototyping
- Prioritization Techniques
- MoSCoW
- Time Boxing
- Balanced Scorecard

- Acceptance and Evaluation Criteria
- Collaborative Games
- Unified Modelling Language, i.e., UML (Use Cases, Activity Diagram, State Diagram, Class Diagram & Sequence Diagram)
- Data Dictionary
- Lessons Learned
- Process Management
- Data Modelling (ER Diagram/Class Diagram/Data Flow Diagram)
- Non-Functional Requirements Analysis
- Metrics and Key Performance Indicators (KPI)s
- Surveys or Questionnaires
- Vendor Assessment
- Solution Assessment
- Change Management
- Decision Analysis
- Traceability Matrix/Item tracker
- Backlog Management
- Reviews
- Requirement Management
- Templates

[* Detailed explanations are provided about each strategy in respective sections.]

Business Analyst's Tools

- Analytics - Google, KISSmetrics, etc. Basic Tool - MS Office, MS Visio and MS Project
- BPMN Modelling - System Archit Note Taking - MS OneNote and Evernote
- Confluence and JIRA Dashboarding - MicroStrategty, Dashthis Data Modelling – ErWin, MS-Visio, Click chart and other free tools General Modelling - Lucidchart and Creately (in absence of MS Visio)
- Data Extract - MicroStrategy ETL, Talend Open Studio, SQL, MongoDB Shells

- EPC Modelling - ARIS
- Invision - combined with Balsamiq (or designs) to make playable demos
- Prototyping - Flinto, Proto.io and iRise
- (IBM) Rational Toolset (it is expensive and not used widely) - ReqPro, Clearcase, Architect, Rose and XDE
- Reporting - Jaspersoft, Tableau
- Wireframing - Balsamiq

These are some of the business analysis techniques available to a business analyst. The business analyst must select the technique(s) based on his and other team members' (involved in a particular activity) comfort, convenience, and organizational culture.

Several other free, as well as licensed tools, are available, depending on one's needs and comfort.

14. What are the Personal Traits required to be a successful business analyst?

The following is a list of the most commonly needed personal traits for a business analyst. A business analyst may require additional skills, depending on the project.

a. Communication: The key aspect of the communication goal must be to forge collaborative relationships, as the active participation of stakeholders is necessary in order to implement the solution successfully. Based on this primary goal, a business analyst can set-up the agenda for communication.

The business analyst needs to have good spoken as well as written communication skills to understand, interpret, and express business requirements in a manner that stakeholders understand them. He should possess good writing skills to communicate with stakeholders, document various artifacts (business need document, business requirement document, vision document, etc.), and reply to queries in a clear, concise, and conflict-free manner. Since a business analyst plays a people-centric role, clarity in his thought process will play a crucial role in ensuring a smooth project management.

b. Analytical Skills: The business analyst needs to possess good analytical skills to understand, analyze, and convert a business need and/or stakeholders' inputs into a specific business requirement. This can be achieved by analyzing various input documents such as user interviews, existing process flows, process documents, etc. A business analyst can make use of use case diagrams, visualizations, SWOT analysis, etc. as techniques to analyze requirements.

c. Critical Thinking: Critical thinking is essential for a business analyst to evaluate multiple options in any given situation and choose the most appropriate one to meet the business objective. For example, a doctor will diagnose the patient's symptoms and history and other appropriate data before deciding on the most suitable treatment. Critical thinking helps the business analyst to continue evaluating various requirements to get to the crux of the actual requirement.

d. Problem Solving: Since the business analyst interacts with different stakeholders and team members, he needs to have good problem-solving skills. He should be able to obtain a 360-degree view of a problem from both technical and business perspectives and should be able to derive a solution that meets a business requirement and technical viability.

e. Attention to Detail: The business analyst processes a vast amount of data and, therefore, attention to detail is a very crucial quality. He should be in a position to articulate requirements in a clear and detail-oriented manner to avoid any ambiguity in requirements.

f. Team Player/Management: Since the business analyst works with various stakeholders, he needs to be a good team player to effectively implement the solution to ensure the project's success. A good team player ensures collaborative working environment, amicable resolution of conflicts, support for the business object, and a shared sense of ownership for the team's goals.

g. Relationship Building: Throughout the solution development lifecycle, the business analyst has to collaborate with various stakeholders, such as customers, management, testers, developers, etc. Hence, it is essential that he is able to build an effective relationship with all the stakeholders. This is to ensure a smooth communication and collaboration for business analysis activities to garner necessary support for requirement management.

h. Influencing: The business analyst needs to have a positive influence on the stakeholders to enable him to achieve objectives of the business analysis. This helps the team to contribute positively towards the objectives and accept the business analyst's ideas with the least resistance.

i. Leadership Qualities: The business analyst acts as a conduit between the business community and technology team. He should be able to motivate and influence the team towards achieving of the business objective.

j. Understanding of Organizational Dynamics: The business analyst needs to have a good understanding of the political environment and organizational dynamics affecting the product to anticipate any challenges it may face. Organizational dynamics involve organizational structure, various business units, business models, key stakeholders, etc. Understanding the organizational dynamics enables the business analyst to understand organizational relationships and politics.

k. Poise: The business analyst needs to display self-confidence in dealing with various stakeholders. He should be able to take the initiative in carrying out his activities with confidence and zeal. Using hard data and factual information, he should be in a position to instill confidence into stakeholders to garner support for the business analysis activities.
[Paul, Cadle, 2011] [Jane, 2016] [Pohl, Rupp, 2011]

15. What are the Career Choices available for a qualified business analyst?

There are many flavors to business analysis, and the business analyst can opt for any one of them depending on his academic and professional background.

The followings are some of the career paths a business analyst can choose from:

Operations Head: A business analyst who manages the business process partially or wholly to improve overall operations by examining their current products, services, processes, and operations to recommend the solution (with or without IT) for improving the business.

Enterprise or Business Architect: A business analyst starting a career as a business analyst, and moving towards lead business analyst and heading business analysis activities as an enterprise or business architect in the organization.

Chief Technology Officer (CTO)/ Chief Operating Officer (COO): In rare cases, this is another possible avenue for a business analyst if the person comes from a technology background. He will have to work through many technology roles such as in-charge of IT projects and overall technology in a non-IT firm to become CTO. This path is suitable for business analysts who have worked their way from business analyst towards program manager, and later to head of operations. A COO is responsible for either business change within the overall business or a specified business division.

Product Owner: A business analyst working in a software company with a specialization in product development can become product owner by working as a product analyst or product manager.

Practice Head: In-charge of projects with the similar domain in a non-IT firm with a mandate to establish processes and standards for business analysis activities such as creating a center of excellence for business analysis.

Program Manager: A business analyst from a business or technical background can manage a portfolio of projects in the same domain in an IT or non-IT Company.

Delivery Head: A business analyst who builds his career path from a technical background and is in-charge of delivering projects or IT services. Delivery head roles could be in an IT or non-IT company within the same or different domains.

Management Consultant: A business analyst is starting as a junior consultant and then going on to progressively become a consultant, senior consultant, and management consultant. [Jane, 2016]

16. What are the Academic/Professional Certifications available to business analysts?
OR
Provide the details of Academic or Professional Training and Certification in the field of business analysis.

There are a few independent organizations that offer professional certificates as mentioned below:

a. Project Management Institute, USA (PMI),
i.   PBA

b. (https://www.pmi.org/certifications/types/business-analysis-pba)

c. International Institute of Business Analysis, Canada (IIBA)
i.   ECBA (Entry Certificate in Business Analysis)
ii. CCBA (Certification of Capability in Business Analysis)
iii. CBAP (Certified Business Analysis Professional)
iv. CBATL (Certified Business Analysis Thought Leader)

For more information, please visit the website. (http://www.iiba.org/Certification-Recognition/certificationlevels.aspx)

d. British Computer Society, UK (BCS),
i.   Certificate in Business Analysis
ii. International Diploma in Business Analysis
iii. Advance Diploma in Business Analysis
iv. Expert BA Award

For more information please visit the website. (https://www2.bcs.org/certifications/ba/)

e. International Requirement Engineering Board, Germany (IREB),
i.   CPRE – FL
ii. CPRE – AL
iii. CPRE – EL

For more information please visit the website (https://www.ireb.org/en/cpre/)

i.   ANISAN Technologies Inc., USA (ANISAN)

ANISAN offers training as well as certification to business analysts at all the levels.
a. CBA Certified Business Analyst)
b. Workshop in Business Analysis
c. Advance Certificate in Business Analysis

For more information, please visit the website.
(http://anisans.com/education-businessanalysis.php)

Several leading universities in the US and UK offer master's degrees, with a major in either Business Analysis, Process Management or Business Transformation.

Some of the leading academic courses in Business Analysis as mentioned below:

a. The University of Manchester
i. Master of Science (MSc) in Business Analysis
(http://www.manchester.ac.uk/study/masters/courses/list/09839/msc-business-analysis-and-strategic-management/)

b. Victoria University of Wellington
i. Master of Professional Business Analysis
(http://www.victoria.ac.nz/sim/study/postgraduate/business-analysis)

c. City University of Hong Kong
i. BBA in Business Analysis
(https://www.cb.cityu.edu.hk/ms/bbabanl/)

17. What are the relevant professional courses available in business analysis?

In the early 2000s, it was relatively easier to enter into the business analyst role without undergoing any professional training. However, the situation has changed due to increased competition and availability of plenty of trained, certified, and experienced business analysis professionals in the job market. Therefore, without professional training and certification, aspiring business analysts may lose out to competitors.

Formal "training" and "certification" definitely helps business analysts in acquiring focused knowledge and skill in the area from an experienced professional.

Although some aspiring business analysts may underestimate the importance of professional training, but a hiring manager will not. The hiring manager will prefer someone who is already equipped with adequate knowledge and skills acquired through professional training to someone who isn't because companies save time and resources in training the new joiner. It also helps to reduce the learning curve after starting in the job.

Most of my students have MBA degrees, and an additional business analysis certificate enables them to compete in the job market more effectively.

a. Better Recognition: It provides recognition of your skills and competence for doing a job, which will allow you to justify your experience and improve employability.

b. Better Career Plan: It helps to build a systematic career plan and advancement strategy.

c. Better Alternate Options: Professional certifications provide an affordable and focused alternate to the university education that many can't afford due to their high cost and longer time schedule.

d. Better Knowledge and Skills: Professional certifications focus on the fundamentals and ensure that the certificate holder acquires the minimum knowledge and skills in the related area.

e. Better Investment for Organization: The hiring manager would find it more beneficial as the company can save time and money in training the prospective employee.

f. Better Skilled Employees/Quality for Organization: The professional certification of employees will validate the company's ability to assign knowledgeable and skilled professionals on the project. Sometimes the clients insist that consultants or employees on their project must have the professional certification to ensure high-quality delivery.

g. Value of Certificate: Reputation of certification awarding body is important. Currently IIBA and BCS are both highly recognized organizations in the field of business analysis. Although PMI is more recognized and offering PMI-PBA, it has limited focus in terms of business analysis. However, academic degrees offered by colleges or universities usually have more formal recognition in a professional assessment. For example, if a professional intends to migrate to another country for the job, the immigration department would give more weightage to a university degree.

h. Better Productivity: It adds to increased engagement, employment satisfaction, and productivity, which are the top ways of measuring the value of professional certification, as they contribute to reductions in staff churn, training, and recruitment costs.

i. Staying Updated: Re-certification ensures that the professionals stay updated in their chosen field.

18. What is the context of business analysis?
Many terminologies used in the business analysis in academic or in the professional world are interpreted in a context. For example, a solution word will have multiple interpretations. However, in business analysis, it is used for a solution to either a business problem or business goal. In

some places, it is explicitly mentioned as "business solution". Requirements are taken into the context of the solution the business analyst is working on as also taken in the context of solution scope.

Value of requirements or the solution is explicitly considered as what value a particular requirement will have in a solution in terms of benefits it delivers.

Solution value is in the context of what value a solution will deliver to the organization regarding financial and non-financial benefits on a long-term basis. This value must consider the initial investment, potential risk, and organizational goals against projected return during its lifetime.

19. What is a Requirement?

In terms of business analysis, it is interpreted as:
    a.   What an organization needs?
    b.   What stakeholders need?
    c.   What teams must do to achieve them?
    d.   What are the conditions, capabilities and constraints a team must follow in providing solution?

Organization needs: This can be interpreted through high-level requirements that align with an organization's goal, mission and objectives. For example, the organization's objectives could be reducing manpower and increasing efficiency by automating the reporting system. This can directly be aligned with the organization's goal to reduce the manpower by 10%, and increase efficiency by reducing turnover time to achieve better results.

These high-level organization's requirements must be elaborated and structured into Terms of Reference (ToR) or a business need document. This document provides an overview of business change.

Stakeholder's Needs: These are individual stakeholders' needs in achieving the organizational common goal and objectives. For example, the marketing team looks at bringing out product wise, region wise, and individual store wise sales reports, while the compliance team wishes to send the sales tax details on an entire sale to the tax authority in the pre-defined format mentioned in government's tax policy document.

So a team working on business change must consider these requirements as it goes about building a report-generating tool or entire system.

Now, when it comes to building the solution that will fulfill the above-mentioned needs, the business analyst must elaborate and structure these business and stakeholder requirements in business requirement documentation, i.e., BRD. It may also be referred to as a product roadmap.

Solution Requirements: These are system requirements. They are specified in terms of functional (specific functionality of the system), quality or non-functional (system performance, security, reliability, etc.), and the system constraints of the solution in a requirement document. An individual requirement or requirement catalogue or collection of requirements in template (functional requirement document, i.e., functional requirement documents (FRD) is also known as a requirement. The IEEE definition summarizes the above description as: "1. a condition or capability needed by a user to solve a problem or achieve an objective. 2. a condition or capability that must be met or possessed by a system or system component to satisfy a contract, standard, specification, or other formally imposed document. 3. a documented representation of a condition or capability as in (1) or (2)" [IEEE, 1998]

Requirements can range from high-level abstract statements of services or system capability and constraints to detailed arithmetical calculation functional specifications.

Requirements Engineering is the process of establishing the facilities that the user requires from the system and the constraints under which the system will be developed and operated.

Requirements may serve a dual function:
- As the basis of a bid for a contract
- As the basis for the contract itself

If an organization desires to outsource the implementation of the system to an external IT vendor, it must do its due diligence before signing the contract that defines details of requirements of the potential system. These details can be features, functionalities, regulatory needs, system capability, pre-defined quality, time to deliver, business and system constraints, operating requirements, etc. The IT vendor may provide details of what potential system can do regarding fulfilling the requirements mentioned previously. At times, a system may be capable of producing the functionally in part or more than what is specified, those constraints are documented as a part of the contract. For example, the specified requirement is to export the report in Excel format and the IT vendor can provide the capability of exporting the report into Excel, PDF, and image format. It will be part of the updated contract, and this contract will serve as the basis of requirement document throughout the project lifecycle.

[Davis, 1993] [IEEE, 1993] [BABOK V2, 2009] [Sommerville, 2003]

20. Who are the Stakeholders and what is their role in the solution development?

A stakeholder is an individual, group, or organization that holds a stake in the solution either partially or wholly. In other words, a stakeholder is anyone who has an interest, stake, or concern in the potential solution because he can either influence or be affected by it.

The one who can influence can either guide or provide expert judgment to optimize the solution. The one who is affected can either provide requirements that need to be incorporated so that they can either continue to perform their role effectively or provide inputs so the solution can be implemented successfully.

The contribution from stakeholders may not be limited to the definition of the solution or requirements, but across all the phases of solution development life cycle through guidance, requirements, requirement management activities, experts' inputs, and reviews to ensure meaningfulness and utility of the potential solution to relevant stakeholders.

In project management, they may be from the business, risk, compliance or technical aspects to ensure everyone's opinion is considered.

The following is a list of partial stakeholders in a project.

Sponsors: The one who sponsors the project. He is the person who assesses the cost vs. benefits and benefit vs. risk before agreeing to fund the project.

System owners: Other system owners with whom the potential system will communicate. They need to be consulted to understand the nature of communication.

Subject Matter Experts (SME): Subject Matter Experts either from business (specific roles such as process owners, auditors, regulators) or from technical (specific roles such as production support, data modeller, or network/infrastructure person, etc.)

Business Analyst: Responsible for defining the solution and managing requirements.

Project Manager: The one who manages and controls project management activities, including project scheduling, budgeting, and allocation of resources.

Testers: The one who tests requirements and solutions.

Technical Lead: A person who leads the technical team developing the solution.

Users: An individual or group (internal or external) that will utilize the solution in future. Their needs must be incorporated to make the solution meaningful and successful.

External Stakeholders: They may be users, SMEs, customers, or vendors using the solution. The SME can be a consultant or an expert in a particular field. [Freeman, 2010]

21. What is the difference between the roles of a project manager and business analyst?

The project manager is in-charge of overall development and successful implementation of a project. The role involves resource management (technical team), schedule management and budget management throughout the project lifecycle. Besides, the project manager is also responsible for risk and issue management, status, and any other technical issues that may arise during the project life cycle.

The project manager also supports the business analyst in defining business needs, solution scope, business case (cost vs. benefit analysis) and feasibility study by providing the required technical data for analysis as well as technical guidance at the initial stage of the project. At a later stage, the project manager or technical team member represents in requirement-elicitation process to guide the team on technical issues and other details. In change management, the project manager involves his team in impact analysis (impact on schedule and budget) and monitoring of the overall project.

While the business analyst on the business side is involved in strategy analysis, such as defining the business needs, determining the solution scope with the help of project manager, preparing a feasibility study and defining business case (cost vs. benefit analysis or ROI) before the project gets the initial go or no-go.

After obtaining the initial go-ahead, the business analyst analyzes and recommends the solution through rigorous requirement elicitation, analysis, documentation and solution assessment processes.

The business analyst on the business side monitors and controls the project by coordinating and guiding the project manager on the IT side.

The business analyst on the IT side analyzes the business and stakeholder requirements (Business Requirement Document (BRD) or Product Roadmap) and transfers them into solution requirements (functional, non-functional, and transition) using standard document structure, templates, and models to elaborate requirements and improve the requirements understandings.

The business analyst supports and collaborates with the business stakeholder and technical team during the entire system development, i.e., through development, testing and implementation phases. He also coordinates and collaborates with business representatives or end-users to conduct User Acceptance Testing (UAT) to ensure that the solution meets user expectations, and also resolves any issues arising during the exercise to help deliver high-quality products.

2. Ideas and Strategy

Collaboration is important not just because it's a better way to learn. The spirit of collaboration is penetrating every institution and all of our lives. So, learning to collaborate is part of equipping yourself for effectiveness, problem solving, innovation and life-long learning in an ever-changing networked economy.

- Don Tapscott

2.1 Strategy Analysis

22. What is a Strategy?
The word "strategy" is derived from the Greek word stratçgos, which further derives from two words stratos meaning army, and ago, which is the ancient Greek for leading, guiding, or moving. In the modern corporate environment, a strategy could be used while planning to launch a new product, revamping an existing product, managing operations, and providing maintenance and customer services.

A strategy can have different meanings in different contexts.
- Goal/Mission of Business: Here, it means the direction or reference for planning and implementing any action(s).
- Timeframe: Here, it means the time allotted to a project - short-term or long-term.
- Resource Optimization: Hiring and managing employees as well as expertise for achieving the organizational goal/mission.
- Environment: An organization's internal and external standards for all activities undertaken internally.

According to the BCS definition of the term, "Strategy is the direction and scope of an organization over the long term, which achieves the advantage for the organization through its configuration of resources within a changing environment and to fulfill stakeholder expectations."

23. What is a Strategy Analysis in the business analysis domain?
Strategy analysis means "the direction and scope of an organization over the long-term, which achieves the advantage for the organization from the configuration of resources within a changing environment and to fulfill stakeholder expectations." [Paul, Yeats et el 2010]

Strategy analysis includes analysis of business needs, including problems or opportunities. Current state, future state, gap analysis, process analysis, solution scope analysis, cost vs. benefit (Return on Investment (ROI)) analysis, domain specific, etc. are all used in defining the business need, solution scope and business case.

Pre-elicitation: Pre-elicitation of strategy analysis involves understanding and defining the problem or the opportunity the business has in the form of a business need, defining a solution scope at a high level, and defining a business case. A business case consists of cost vs. benefit analysis i.e. analysis of cost as investment vs. benefits (the tangible and non-tangible) the solution offers during its life. Also, the benefits (the tangible and non-tangible) vs. risk (business and operations) analysis the organization may face following implementation of business change. It also involves understanding the project's complexity and novelty to determine the most appropriate project approach to define business analysis deliverables, identify stakeholders and understand their nature of collaboration.

Outlining the strategy of dealing with data generated during the project, policies related to requirement management, details needed in handling such requirements and understanding of relevant data about requirements management, including creating repositories, assigning values, establishing structures, and prioritizing requirements are also important part of the pre-elicitation process.

Post-elicitation: Post-elicitation of strategy analysis involves examination of the defined solution (Business Requirement Document or Product Roadmap) against an organization's current and future capability and gaps, if any. It also verifies if the defined solution addresses the business need (problems or opportunities) and its feasibility. The defined solution scope is confirmed against the organizational scope to understand if it covers the basic scope and is in-line with the organization's current and future goals and objectives. In addition, it also assesses the possible solution approaches (buying an off-the-shelf product or building a customized solution). This analysis, in part or whole, is also referred to as enterprise analysis in some of the books on the subject.

Post-transition: This analysis aims to verify if the transitioned solution addresses the problem or the opportunity defined in the business need. It also checks the possible options available for enhancement and enrichment of the solution during its lifecycle.

2.2 Business Need

24. What is a Business Need?

Every organization, irrespective of its type (public, private, government, or non-profit) or nature of its respective business, serves people through its vision, mission and goal(s).

Throughout its life cycle, an organization creates and updates its business goals, objectives, and business needs in response to its business, market, and customers' situation or demand. The business need helps to achieve those business objectives.

The "business need" in business analysis is either a problem or an opportunity that an organization addresses in order to fulfill its goals and objectives.

Business Need – Problem: This entails fixing the existing problems in the areas of business or technology and achieving the business objectives such as increasing customer or employee satisfaction. These could be the challenges arising out of repeated and cumbersome work. Also, it can be a decreased operational cost that would be addressed by removing operational pain points or ensuring faster delivery of goods and services through the introduction of new RFID warehouse solutions or removing redundant processes.

In addition to the above, these could be employed to fulfill the newly introduced set of rules or changes to existing regulatory requirements, align a current business process or operation with new organizational standards, and generate new reports to enable an effective decision-making process.

The problems are typically reported through a bottom-up (the users reporting to their manager) or peer-to-peer (a manager reporting to other manager who is in-charge of business unit or that part of business operations) approach.

Business Need – Opportunity: The objectives could be to increase profitability by automating manual processes, increasing brand value, and introducing new products or services or both.

The management typically strategizes opportunities either through a top-down or peer-to-peer approach.

Stakeholders or business analysts first understand a problem or opportunity and its likely impact on business, and then proceed for defining and documenting these business needs efficiently.

It forms the basis to commence work on a new solution.

25. What factors must a business analyst understand while preparing a Business Need Document?

While writing about the business need (problems or opportunities), a business analyst must understand the source of the problem, and the impact of the problem on people, processes, business units, and functionalities. He is required to collaborate with the business and the technical teams, including the project manager, to define the possible solution and scope after considering current market standards.

A business analyst must keep everyone in the loop while defining the business need document as it is required to consider the legal, operational, technical, and business issues along with the assumptions and constraints (both business and technical) before presenting it to the sponsor.

The business need document should be comprehensive, correct, and complete as it serves as the basis to project planning and management activities.

Defining Business Need: Either a Problem or an Opportunity)

To do this, the business analyst can follow the below steps with respect to establishing the current state (As-Is) and future state (To-Be).

Understanding the Business:

<u>a. Business Definition:</u>

A business definition consists of the analysis of following information

I. Type of Entity: What is the entity type? Is it a proprietary, public limited, cooperative, government, body corporate or not-for-profit organization? This definition will help in understanding the style of functioning depending on the regulations, accounting standards, etc.

II. Business Domain: A business domain could be agriculture, service, hospitality, defense, health care, banking, retail, manufacturing, and logistics. It helps a business analyst to understand the nature of an industry and its specific requirements.

III. Products and Services: This involves listing out of all the products and services offered. It helps in further refining industry details. For example, in the hospitality sector, a 5-star hotel and 5-star resort owned by the same firm will have different operational requirements owing to different nature of services offered.

IV. Organizational Structure: Interconnectedness between organizational units and sub-units, and their communication with the central entity/head office. It will provide the details of the organization's work culture, operations, and communication.

V. Organization Structure: This will specify employee structure and their association with entities, and their role and position in the organizational hierarchy.

VI. Management Culture: Is it democratic, lean, hierarchical, traditional or modern? In addition, the details of policies and processes, such as quality policy and standards, quality management processes, and values and belief systems.

VII. Clients/Customers and Market: It is pertinent to understand who the clients and customers are, and what their specific needs are. For example, the customer banking with a local bank and the customer banking with an international bank will have very diverse backgrounds and requirements. Although both banks are part of the same industry, their operational structure will be completely different due to the profile of the customers they are serving.

VIII. Operational, Legal and Compliance Requirements: This will specify how the products and services reach the end customers. What are the main processes? Who and what are their customers, industry and regulatory standards in delivering these services? For example, are bank customers able to complete the transaction over the Internet or are physically required to visit a branch? Moreover, since they are regulated by a federal bank and other legal and regulatory requirements, will any of these regulations affect the process or product that are being defined? If yes, the business analyst will have to consider these as additional needs.

IX. Organizational Goals: What are an organization's long-term and short-term goals, and how are they linked to its current business needs? This information helps in providing a vision of the solution.

X. Core Competence: This provides the focus area in terms of products and services. For instance, why does a particular product sell better compared to its peers? What is and what is not appreciated about it? We also need to probe if any other specific products, services or issues need to be considered in the scope analysis.

XI. Competitive Stand: Who are your nearest competitors? Compare your stand against three levels up and three levels down to find out how you compare with them.

b. External Influence:

I. Industry Benchmark: The business analyst, along with market research analyst, will have to understand the industry standards in terms of products, processes, and quality. For example, in the IT industry, the Capability Maturity Model Integration (CMMi) level for processes will be of International Organization for Standardization (ISO) standards.

II. Current and Potential Future Trends: This data will support building long-life futuristic solutions. The longer the solution is used, the more beneficial it is as it delays the cost of replacing or updating the solution, thereby delivering more value on the investment.

III. New Regulations: Study of new regulations will ensure that the proposed solution is compliant with them, with no additional requirements or fixes required at a later stage.

All this information and data is very useful in analyzing a business in a comprehensive manner. Without this analysis, the business analyst cannot provide the most appropriate solution.

c. Technology:
Introduction of technology in the industry and its influence on the existing solution may threaten the brand value, customer service, or overall business. [Jane, 2016]

26. When we identify the Problem or the Opportunity, what are the Activities to be considered?

Once we have identified the problem or opportunity, we have the following areas to work on:

a. History:
History of the problem or opportunity

b. Source:
The source of the problem or opportunity

c. Background:
How the opportunity has arisen or been generated

d. Impact analysis:

Impact analysis mean identifying business value or Business Impact Analysis (BIA)

- Area (department, functions, etc.): This constitutes part of the organization or functions it is affecting. Or it could be one "field" or multiple fields. For example, if the problem is in retrieving sales data for a retail chain, we will have to check if the problem is in a part of the region or across it. Or it could be within one or multiple "fields".

- Stakeholders: These include users, customers, and the penultimate signing-off authority. To what extent are they directly or indirectly affected? Are a higher number of stakeholders impacted by the problem or opportunity? The nature of impact should be considered before the business need is fully defined.

Note: Please refer to stakeholder analysis in the planning phase for more details.

- Business Operations: Where is the impact? Is it a single process or the entire gamut of business processes that is affected? Is it industry-wide impact? For example, change in service tax rates may affect the pricing and accounting process of an organization. Whereas implementation of an internationally binding regulation like Basel II and Basel III affects the entire banking universe.

- The best way to approach the problem is to complete the "gap analysis", where existing business processes or an operating model are compared against new (required) business processes and the organization's current and future capability requires implementing the same.

- Financial and non-financial impact of the proposed solution
- Will it increase revenue?
- Will it decrease expenses?
- Will it bring in new customers?
- Will it bring in more money from existing customers?
- Will it improve employee morale?

Not all problem-solving leads to business value, such as financial and brand value. Sometimes resolving problems may result in improving processes that make things easier for employees in areas, such as accessing of data to make well-informed decisions.

Redundant, lengthy, and cumbersome processes can be improved to make it easier for employees to perform their routine tasks without having to seek additional approvals. This may result in improving employee morale, with additional challenging project/work in their professional life.

e. Brand and Image Impact:
Problem within existing products or services or problems related to customers or problems related to operations, i.e., delivery of products or services to end customers.

- Will it increase shareholder or taxpayer value? Increased customer satisfaction or improved products of services may result in increased revenue. Reduction in operational costs could result in increased revenue. In both the cases, there will be a direct or indirect impact on shareholder value.

f. Policy, Legal, and Compliance:
Any new compliance or policy change may result in change in existing operations or need for new business operations. Either way, it may result in the business need for new business systems.

g. Recommendations:
Recommending Possible Options to Resolve the Problem: The business analyst works in collaboration with stakeholders on the possible solutions that can be aligned with goals set to deal with the problem.

- Setting up realistic expectations in dealing with the problem.
The objectives or outcome of the solution must be in-line with resolving the problem or taking care of the identified opportunity.

- The objectives must be fulfilled when these expectations are met after implementing the business solution or a project.

- It must be explicitly stated, "The data migration must be completed by July 31 of the said year." This goal must be well communicated and agreed upon by all concerned, i.e., stakeholders, sponsors and team members.

- The goal must be logical, reasonable, and doable.

- Verify and validate the problem definition with the affected people, stakeholders, and existing processes and policies.

- Confirm and sign-off the problem definition.

For example, if your firm intends to streamline technology across the organization or it wishes to upgrade its business solution to the latest and best ones available in order to provide faster, effective, and more secured solutions to improve both its customer service and competitive advantage.

- Verify, validate, and redefine (whenever necessary) the business need.

- Align the business need: Ensure that the outcome of this exercise, i.e., the business need actually aligns with your organization's goals and objectives. For example, if operational costs are required to be reduced by up to 15%, check if there is a need for either process improvement or re-engineering. Or another classic example could be providing value-added services to the existing range of products to expand the customer base by up to 10% within a year of implementing the solution.

- The defined business need clearly explains the problem area or opportunity for the organization. For example, 30% percent of users of a particular e-commerce website have complaints about their overall experience while shopping online. They further state that compared to other similar websites, it is relatively difficult to use.

- Ensure that the final version of business need has achieved stakeholder consensus and is supported by valid data, trends or analysis.

27. What are the components of a Business Need Document? Also, describe these components.

TABLE OF CONTENTS

1	Introduction
2	Purpose of the Business Needs Statement Document
3	General Information
4	Investment/Project Description
5	APPENDIX A: BUSINESS NEEDS STATEMENT APPRO
6	APPENDIX B: REFERENCES
	APPENDIX C: KEY TERMS

Introduction

The purpose of the online banking solution document is to define the problem or idea, and it may acquire the form of a potential project. It includes a problem or an opportunity, its impact, a high-level scope, and its alignment with business goals. The solution scope includes estimated schedule and cost. The comprehensive scope is described in a vision and mission document.

We will now examine how this problem or opportunity will fulfill current and future goals of internal and external stakeholders.

The business need statement describes sufficient details that offer an overview of the project and provides justification for the "go" or "no-go" decision to the next level, i.e., the elaboration of the full-fledged business case. If the proposed solution is required to fulfill any regulatory requirement, the document needs to highlight the details of the consequences of not implementing them.

General Information

Date Requested	<mm/dd/yyyy>
Requested By	<Enter full name>

Email	<Enter email address>
Phone	<000-000-0000>
CO/CC	<Enter CO/CC>
Business Owner	<Enter Business Owner/Manager supporting this document>

Investment/Project Description

Name	<Enter a name for the potential Solution/Investment>
Preferred Start Date	<Enter a desired start date for the potential Solution/Investment (mm/dd/yyyy)>
Business Need (Problem/Opportunity)	<Enter a detailed description of the business need that the solution is going to address/an idea that is being realized. The details must include the projected benefits from the investment of resources or the risk it poses not being invested into proposed solution or an idea.>
Goals & Objectives/Scope	<Enter a detailed description of the purpose, goals, objectives, and scope of the proposed I/P>
	<How the goals of proposed solution/idea align with organizational goals and objectives.>
Projected Estimation	<Enter projected estimation of proposed solution/an investment in an idea. The estimation may include high-level resource planning. Please support this with business case, if available.
Risks/Issues	<Enter the business, operational, and technical risks of doing, and/or not doing it. Please support the Benefit vs. Risk analysis, if possible.>

Approval

Please present the list of stakeholders whose signatures are required. For examples, their names, designations, role in the project and signatures.

#	Name, and Designation	Role	Signature
1	Ms. Veena Deshmukh, Business Analyst	Author	
2	Mr. Morgan Smith, Business Analyst	Reviewer	

Reference

Please provide the reference documents used to prepare this business need document. [Name, Version Number, Description, and Location]

Glossary

Please provide key terms or glossary used in this document.

#	Key terms	Description /Definition
	SME	Subject Matter Experts

[CDC.gov]

2.3 Stakeholder Analysis

Identification of stakeholders and their role within a project began in the 1990s.

Around that time, the main emphasis was put into identifying the stakeholders as software solutions started getting complex and integrated with the introduction of advanced technology to accommodate the latest business dynamics. With this development, the solutions were now not only required to cater to project sponsors but also stakeholders, whose roles or systems were affecting the existing processes directly or indirectly. However, failing to comply with the needs of other relevant stakeholders, the software solutions started facing major hurdles in finding acceptance among other stakeholders. In some worst-case scenarios, their adaptation triggered intense conflict and confusion. In one reported extreme case at least, Shane Co., a leading jewelry chain, was forced to file for bankruptcy after its SAP solution failed horrendously as it was implemented without either considering the employees' or organization's culture. After some key employees left their jobs in sheer frustration, the second-level managers too left the company, causing a massive deficit in resources to support the operations. This eventually led the company to file for bankruptcy. [Kanaracus, 2009]

Within the field of software engineering in the 1970s and 1980s, the understanding of the term "stakeholder" widened to first the main users of the software solution and then peripheral users. However, in the 1990s, the search for stakeholders took on a far more systemic approach. It came to be increasingly recognized that stakeholders existed in an organization as consultants, vendors, and customers. Other stakeholders included are:

- Those organizations that integrate (or should integrate) horizontally with the organization the analyst is designing the system for
- Any back-office systems or organizations
- Higher management
- Vendors
- End-users
- IT team members (development and operation phase)
- Temporary consultants
- Customers

Successful identification of stakeholders ensures that analysis will take into account the following right elements:
- Identification of stakeholders
- Documentation of stakeholder information pertaining to their roles, responsibilities, skills, special requirements, contact information, authority level, attitude towards project, and influence within the organization and on project.
- Stakeholder collaboration documents details, such as who will participate in what activities at what level and at what stage. It also specifies accommodating the special requirements or additional role that a stakeholder might likely to consider.

This information supports in building business need, solution scope, business case (where the business analyst needs to define scope), collecting data from respective roles and validating the case.

These stakeholders contribute in verifying and validating the solution through defining, analyzing, designing, developing, implementing, and creating a successful collaboration among various teams.

28. What is the Stakeholder Analysis?

Stakeholder analysis is the systematic approach and activity to identify stakeholders and their details (contact details, roles, and responsibilities and their personas) required for the proposed solution.
- Identify your stakeholder.
- Document stakeholder information, such as their roles, responsibilities, skill-sets, unique attributes, authority level, attitude regarding the project, and influence within their organization. Such information will come in handy when you proceed to both defining the scope and collating data from respective roles in order to validate your business case.

Such stakeholders will contribute to reviewing and validating solutions through development and implementation as well as creating a successful collaboration among various teams.

29. How is the stakeholder identified for the proposed solution?
- By studying the business need (problem or an opportunity) and solution scope document to understand stakeholders and their involvement.
- Outlining the stakeholders' details by studying the organizational structure or modelling the organization (enterprise architecture) and their relationships, and communication.
- Getting additional details through existing documents related to stakeholder analysis.
- Communicating and collaborating with identified stakeholders to confirm details thus obtained (except for details on their attitude and persona).

30. How is a Stakeholder Analysis conducted?
The stakeholder analysis is part of the planning activities in the business analysis or requirement management. If the business analyst misses this, he is bound to face several hurdles. Stakeholder analysis is the key to

succeed in a project as missing out on any stakeholder during analysis means that their requirements will add to the project as either an additional requirement or a change requirement in the future.

Consequently, both would have an impact on the project timeline and budget. Moreover, the stakeholder may be disappointed for not including him in the first place.

Let's understand how to work on stakeholder analysis. The following are a few tips for analyzing stakeholders and creating a list in the most effective way.

- By studying the business need (problem or opportunity) and solution scope document to understand stakeholders and their involvement.
- Outlining the stakeholders' details by studying organizational structure or modelling the organization (enterprise architecture) and their relationships and communication.
- Getting additional details through existing documents related to stakeholder analysis.
- Communicating and collaborating with identified stakeholders to confirm details thus obtained (except for details on their attitude and persona).

Process: First, recognize the impact of the business need (problem or an opportunity). Once the business analyst knows the details, those will become the basis for stakeholder analysis. The business analyst can also obtain the organizational structure to understand people and their roles. He can hold a discussion with the main stakeholders to identify them or else can obtain the official stakeholders' list as some organizations have formally designated persons from every department to act as stakeholders.

The business analyst can compile the data in Excel and verify the same with the relevant stakeholders.

GLOBAL BANK LTD (stakeholders List, Role, Responsibility and other description)										
Business Role / User Group	User	Contact Detail	Location	Subject Matter Knowledge	Technical Knowledge	RASCI	Attitude	Influence	Unique Facts	Expectations	Ways to Manage expectations
Milind Shah, CTO		milinds@gbl.com, 022-22991000	Mumbai HO	IT Infrastructure & Security, Enterprise Application, Project Management	IT Infrastructure & Security, Enterprise Application, Project Management	R	5	5	Very particular about details and timelines	Played a major role in convincing management in implementing the solution and hence relates very much to the success of the project	Have to be updated regularly with the status of the project
Ms. Wendy Smith, EVP, Operations		wendys@gbl.com, 022-23994555	Mumbai HO	Bank operations	MS Office	I	4	5	Focus on quality enhancement and profitability.	More interested in synopsis than in details	Ensure that project objectives are clearly stated with respect to enhancement of productivity and profits
Ankush Shah, VP Project Management		ankushs@gbl.com, 022-22991003	Mumbai HO	Project Management, Bank operations	IT Infrastructure & Security, Enterprise Application, Project Management	A	4	4	Had successfully implemented Core Banking Solution for the Bank and has led many other such developmental project	Documentations should be complete and consise	List of various deliverables and resultant documentation tasks and responsibilities to be fixed in next meeting
Daniel Jos, VP, Compliance & Risk		danielj@gbl.com, 022-23994560	Mumbai HO	RBI Regulations, Audit and Compliance.	MS Office	C	3	3	Expectations related to compliance of regulatory requirements and banks internal process requirements are high.	No compromise in terms of regulatory requirements to be met. Solution should be in line with the regulatory requirements.	Meeting fixed to explain how various regulatory requirements are taken care of in te proposed solution and obtain feedback on any ammends required.
Mr. Frank Mayberger, VP Enterprise application		frankm@gbl.com, 02-23991010	Data Centre	Existing banking application	Enterprise Application	S	4	4	Neutral towards new solution	Expects to be updated regularly on project progress	Stakeholder review reports
Mr. Sidney Hart, VP IT Infrastructure and Security;		sidneyh@gbl.com, 02-23991002	Data Centre	IT Infrastructure & Security, Project Management	IT Infrastructure & Security	S	4	4	Already involved in other technology initiatives	Prior meeting appointment and agenda to be set for any guidance required	Obtained secretary details and taken note for meeting with appointments
Mary Fedrick, VP Retail		maryf@gbl.com, 022-2399462	Central Processing	Retail Banking	MS Office	C	3	4		New solution should enchance the effectiveness of the	Presentation organised outlining the detailed benefits to the

The RACI is mentioned as below.

R	Responsible	C	Consulted
A	Accountable	I	Informed
S	Supported		

Attitude	0-5 (5 is the highest positive)
Influence	0-5 (5 is the highest influencing ability)

Attitude 0-5 (5 is the highest positive)
Influence 0-5 (5 is the highest influencing ability)

- Influence *
- Attitude *

The data can be compiled using following parameters.
- # / Stakeholder Number
- Name
- Contact Details (Contact Number, Email)

- Location
- Role and Responsibilities
- Authority Level
- Profile
- Technical Skills /Proficiency
- Preferred Environment
- Special Needs
- RACI (R - Responsible, A - Accountable, C - Consulted and I Informed. Some may add S for Support, but that is optional)
- Additional Description
- Group/Category

Please note that the data or column for attitude and influence are only for your reference to build your strategy with the stakeholders in the future, unless you want to invite trouble. This information will provide you with the requisite details to make the project successful.

 # / Stakeholder Number: A unique identifier associated with a particular stakeholder and his records.

Name and Contact Details: This information collected at the beginning of the project will provide you a reference base for your communication planning. This single point document helps you to avoid the unnecessary struggle of trying to obtain a stakeholder's contact information at the last minute.

Location: Location information is an additional data related to the stakeholder's time zone that is useful in planning for virtual meetings or telephonic discussions and travel arrangements. This is especially helpful if you are organizing an interpersonal meeting or workshop.

Role and Responsibilities: This will help you to collect appropriate data from stakeholders based on their individual expertise level. The role and authority level will contribute to defining what information you can collect in certain areas. For example, an operations person will provide you with details about the process and daily troubles in the long run. Since he is working on the process, he can efficiently identify the current and future bottlenecks as well as possible solutions for the changes to make it better. The department head will provide you with the policies related to organizational culture and standards in future change. They may even approach the senior management if any policy matter needs to be changed on an urgent or a long-terms basis.

Authority Level: This indicates the organization's internal hierarchy.

Profile: This describes the details of profile of the stakeholder if it is unique or needs explanation.

Technical Skills/Proficiency: The stakeholder's individual technical proficiency.

Preferred Environment: This describes the stakeholder's preference for working in a particular technical environment or using certain tools.

Special Needs: This describes any special needs the stakeholders may have and that cannot be specified under any other attribute.

RACI: This will help you in categorizing the stakeholders and getting a clearer picture about their involvement in future projects. Please see the next question for more details.

Attitude and Influence: A stakeholder's attitude is based on people who are involved in the project at various levels.

Project Manager and His Core Team: Any setbacks faced by the project in the past, its inability to generate adequate confidence in stakeholders, presence of inflated or insufficient confidence and lack of transparency across stages could introduce negativity into the mind of a stakeholder for future projects.

Another reason why a stakeholder may not be on good terms with the project initiator is that the former might never possibly want the project initiator to succeed. There are various reasons why the stakeholder may not have a good view about the project.

This information will help you to build a strategy at the early stages to garner more support and build a positive image of your project. The most important part of the project is the user satisfaction in using the project. To maximize that, the analyst must work on getting active participation of stakeholders from an early stage to define the project scope. However, this data must remain confidential.

Description or Comments: Add one more column to record additional information that won't fit into any of the previous categories. These details will come in handy in soliciting inputs to make the project successful.

An analyst must remember that this document is started when a business need is arisen and defined at the initial stage. This is a key document to delimit the scope of the project and serves as a base to plan detailed communication and activities, explain high-level requirements and elaborate stakeholders' expectation throughout the project. Poorly compiled or outdated information in this document may jeopardize the project where it impacts a vital requirement or feature if the key stakeholder is either omitted or wrongly defined.

The analyst must confirm details on this information (except attitude and influence) from a relevant stakeholder to avoid future misconceptions and/or misunderstandings.

An authorized person must update the document to avoid complications such as any loss of data or track of changes. [Jane, 2016]

You can add more parameters to this and create a matrix that can be easily used.

31. What is RACI?

RACI is stakeholder analysis technique or matrix to understand the possible nature of involvement of the stakeholder in solution development.

It stands for:

R – Responsible (A person who is responsible in completing the activities partially or completely. For example, a business analyst is responsible for defining the requirements)

A – Accountable (A person who is accountable for decisions made and accountable for the success/failure of the overall project. For example, a sponsor will be held accountable for the success or failure of the project.)

C – Consulted (A person whose involvement is necessary to inform and confirm requirement or project management decisions. For example, for any new requirement proposed, the business analyst will consult the project manager to understand the feasibility, impact and other technical details before making a decision.)

I – Informed (A person who is not directly involved, but his work will be impacted if any changes are made to the requirements or project. For example, a data modeller is informed if there are any changes to the requirement, so he can incorporate those changes into the database.)

Some prefer to use the additional parameter, "S" for "Supported" if needed.

Therefore, it could also be RACIS.

The SMEs support the project manager and business analyst in comprehending necessities and needs of business users or stakeholders' likes or interests. These could be how the project helps save time on transactions, how much security is required per application or its long-term profitability. The SMEs explain how the stakeholders or business users want the application, to be or appear to be for the customers or business users.

32. Does the IT business analyst directly interact with business stakeholders and why?

This interaction is dependent on a clutch of factors. Typically, an IT business analyst works closely with the project manager in the technology team. The technology team has a communication channel or protocol to follow while interacting with the business stakeholders.

This channel or protocol is possible in an agile or fast-paced environment, as the team gets to work and interact closely.

This also happens when the project team is using a software tool for requirement management and all stakeholders from both the business and technical sides are closely networking on project-related matters.

An IT business analyst may interact with the business stakeholder if the person is deputed at the client location for elicitation or other work.

33. How do you deal with difficult stakeholders?

At times, stakeholders can create an awkward situation. But we can overcome such a situation by:

- Listening actively
- Asking relevant questions and creating interest and understanding
- Speaking to them in their language (domain)
- Being polite and exchanging pleasantries
- In the eventuality of a stressful situation, allow the matter to calm down first
- Sticking to issue-based discussions

- Communicating and collaborating effectively to make stakeholders a part of the solution development process
- Creating a positive and trustworthy environment
- Gaining respect by being sincere towards work and organizational goals

2.4 Gap Analysis

34. How do you define the Current State (As-Is)?

Since the business transformation or change implementation happens in the context of products or services offered by organizations, people (stakeholders), processes, technologies, policies, and data, the business analyst needs to understand and define the current state (As-Is) to help stakeholders visualize the future state (To-Be). The current state description serves as the basis to define the future state (To-Be).

This helps in reducing the effort and improving effectiveness of visualizing and defining the future state. The current state definition will also ensure to considering all requirements in the existing system(s) that are required. In most situations, enhancing and enriching the existing system is preferred to creating something new from scratch.

The current state description in the context of business transformation includes the following organizational information but limited to:

- Organization's product and services
- Organizational structure, polices and culture
- Business operations, architecture, business processes, business rules and regulations
- Current relevant systems, application, desktop tools, technology, data, information and technology infrastructure.
- Details of internal as well as external stakeholders, and other details.
- Internal and external influence factors, including current capabilities, suppliers, regulators, political environment, and economy.
- In addition, the information related to existing problems, regulatory issues and new opportunities that the existing system is incapable of handling also comes in handy.

- Here, it is important to remember to consider previous version or changes made to the Current State (As-Is) in order to get a better insight into it.

Examples of Current State (As-Is)

Current state is defined based on the business need, solution context and novelty of the project. Several parameters are considered to define the current state.

The following are some of the criteria to be considered to describe the current state in context of feature and functionalities:

a. Features and functionalities
   - Manual fund transfer
   - Manual passbook to maintain a bank account record
   - Inter-branch operability
   - Loan (personal, vehicle, home, or business etc.)
   - Investment (mutual fund, SIP, etc.)
   - Fixed Deposit (FD, RD, etc.)
   - Insurance

b. Process
   - Manual payment process by visiting the branch

c. Technology
   - Intranet-based application to update data

35. How do you define the Future State (To-Be)?

The future state (To-Be) is the desired state that an organization and stakeholders wish to achieve in terms of implementing a new or a modified solution or replacing the existing solution in part or wholly. The solution or transformation boundaries may change due to any changes in business due to M&A or selling-off a part of the business.

This information includes the following, but is not limited to:

- Organization's future line of business, i.e., products and services
- Organizational future structure, polices and culture
- Future business operations, architecture, business processes, business rules and regulations
- Future relevant systems, application, desktop tools, technology, data, information and technology infrastructure.
- Future details of the internal as well as the external stakeholders, and other details. These include changed roles and responsibilities, if any.
- Future competencies that includes knowledge and skills of stakeholders, users, customers and suppliers. Also, training required to accommodate future competencies.
- Future internal and external influence factors include the capability and capacity of the organization, customers, and their suppliers, etc. The influencing factors also include the regulators' requirements, changing political environment, or economic trends.
- Other future needs based on market analysis

The future state must be well defined, correct, consistent and complete in nature. It must justify the investment in terms of its potential benefits, such as increase in revenue, increase in customer base, increase in brand value, reduced operational costs, etc. These benefits must be quantifiable as much as possible against the cost to understand if it is doable within the estimated time and budget. Moreover, most stakeholders must support transformation and agree that it aligns with the organization's specified goals and objectives.

The details in terms of cost, potential benefits, and list of associated risks must be clearly listed down if there is more than one option available to achieve the future state.

Example of Future State (To-Be):

The future state of an organization is defined and described based on its current state and future state needs with regards to the solution context and novelty of the project. There are many parameters to be considered to define the future state.

The following are some of the criteria to be considered to describe the future state in the context of the feature and functionalities.

- Features and Functionalities
    o Online Fund Transfer
    o Online Profile Management
    o Online Account (transaction, activities) Statement - View/download
    o e-Services (applying for an IPO, creating e-Card, gift card, etc.)
    o Bill Payments
    o Credit Cards
    o e-Tax Payments
    o Loan (personal, car loan, home loan, business etc.)
    o Investment (Mutual Fund, SIP, etc.)
    o Fixed Deposit (fixed, recurring, etc.)
    o Insurance

- Process
    o Online payment process without interference from the branch

- Technology
    o Internet-based application to update the data online.

36. What is the Gap Analysis? What is the process used for arriving at improvements in processes?

Gap analysis is a formal study to identify the gaps between a business' current capabilities and its future capabilities in terms of performance, processes, reports, regulations, sales, systems, etc. These may be linked to business, technology, and products or services against future capabilities or needs. The study could be restricted to the department's particular function, product or location, or it could also be an enterprise-wide analysis. Gap analysis actually defines the benchmarking of the future portfolios, systems, or processes.

We use gap analysis, i.e., we define As-Is (current state) in terms of current procedures, products, services, and operations, and align them with current goals using various parameters such as processes, questions, metrics, comparative analysis, and market data. We derive the gap in the current-state (As-Is) expected or the future-state (To-Be). Using the result of gap analysis and synthesizing that with future goals and their requirements, we arrive at future state (To-Be), i.e., improvements needed.

Gap Analysis = To-Be (Future State) − As-Is (Current State)

GAP Analysis					
Functionalities or New capabilities	As-Is	To-Be	Gap	Priority	Comments
Operating Model	Current Operating Model	Future Operating Model	Future Capabilities	Medium	Need to achieve the future operating model to keep the pace with future requirements.
Technology	System is in VB 6.0	System to be build in .NET	Technology up gradation	High	Need latest technology to deal with system
Legal / Compliances	Nil	As per the new regulation, the account department needs to implement Sarbane-Oxlay audit process	Incorporate new process or update existing process to implement the accounting regulation	High	Implementation is mandatory requirement.
Industry Standards	Many Competitors have started providing online shopping facilities to the busy customers	Need to provide online shopping facilities in addition to store business	Online shopping system that provide real-time shopping experience.	High	It is important to retain existing customers, add new ones for the growth of future business.
Performance	Old system is unable process more than 50 request in a minutes	Future anticipated request will be the ability of system to handle 500 request in a minutes	Require 10 times faster system		With current and projected growth, the system must cater to be updated to cater to existing and future needs.

| Look and Feel | Outdated site in terms of look and feel, navigations, menus and pictures i.e. outdated website | Need attractive site with updated content, great graphics, navigations and user friendly experience | Updated and user friendly website with advanced features. | Medium | Younger customers are techno-savvy and their expectations are more than what existing system can offer. |

(The enlarged size picture is available on page number 275)

Although the scope of the book is restricted to IT business analysis, we need to discuss this topic in a little more detail so that the Business Analyst can get a detailed perspective of the gap analysis done using scenarios such as:
- Business Process/Industry Standards Analysis
- Products & Services Analysis
- IT Systems Analysis
- Compliance Analysis
- Technology Analysis
- Performances Analysis

Business Process/Industry Standards Analysis:
If an organization decides to improve its overall processes implementing ISO or just adhering to new security (e.g., "VeriSign") requirements to obtain the certification for handling the secured online payments. In both these cases, there could be an impact on the current processes in the respective departments. Thus, gap analysis entails identification and definition of future requirements for the solution.

Products and Services Analysis:
Based on the company's projection, there could be requirements or plans to expand the existing portfolio by adding new products or discontinuing existing product(s). These are very high-level gap analyses that are done by keeping in mind the future growth of the company and consumer needs. Here, the company's profit and shareholder interest are taken into consideration. For example, considering the demand and future need for health foods, Pepsi decided to enter into the segment and acquired the Tropicana brand to expand its portfolio. Market potential, usage gaps,

and competitive gaps are other factors to be considered while undertaking gap analysis.

Compliances Analysis:
Recently, there have been new compliances introduced by financial regulatory bodies such as the Securities and Exchange Commission (SEC) in the US and the Securities and Exchange Board of India (SEBI), as well as other such bodies in other countries. These compliances deal with (possible) financial frauds and are also intended to ease the business process. For example, a change introduced by the SEC was "Locate the stock" in the "Short-Selling" process in 2005 and similarly, in 2010, SEBI, through Mutual Funds Amendment Regulations, introduced new timeframes in conducting the mutual funds business.

Technology Analysis:
The enterprise-wide analysis will facilitate defining the gap between the outdated technology that exists and current and/or future needs of the new technology or machines that will improve the products, services, or operations of a company. For example, offset printing machines vs. digital printing machines with the latest features offered by HP.

In IT, the term "gap analysis" is defined as the detailed study of the gap between future systems or the requirement or process (which is known as 'To-Be', which means the way it should be or "to be") and the current system or process (which is known as "As-Is" i.e., meaning the way "it is" or "as it is").

Performance Analysis:
Performance analysis includes studying performance of the existing pace of current state regarding process, system and people delivering their services internally and externally. This analysis seeks to provide the expected or future state. The "gap" is analyzed, and actions are recommended to bridge it. For example, if an e-commerce business delivers goods in seven to eight business days through a normal domestic shipping mode that is slower than the existing industry standard of five to

six days, its delivery performance, therefore, needs to be improved. [Jane, 2014]

37. How is a Feasibility Study conducted?

How we approach the problem or opportunity is the key part of business solution. Whether or not it is feasible is a separate matter. Therefore, it goes without saying that prior to initiating any business plan, an assessment of its feasibility is a must.

Simply put, the term "feasibility" refers to the goal that is achievable along vital parameters such as market readiness, customer acceptance, technical compatibility with the existing internal as well as external systems, and other technologies integrated with the solutions, such as global positioning system (GPS) or radio frequency identification (RFID).

To illustrate, any kind of online transaction business over a decade ago in India would be tantamount to walking on a tricky terrain. Credit cards were not widely used. Secondly, there were no payment gateways (secured payment processing service providers to the e-commerce businesses who could accept the payment on clients' behalf). Besides, the Internet was an uncharted territory and banks were reluctant to share their customers' data over the Internet or with any third-party payment service providers. The copyright and infringement laws were not as strict, nor were there any state-of-the-art security solutions to guarantee customer privacy.

Today, however, setting up an online business is definitely easier. The widespread use of the credit/debit cards and electronic wallets such as Apple Pay, BHIM (Bharat Interface for Money), Paytm etc., the support provided by the latest technologies to secure the solution, and the stringent data security rules have all facilitated that.

To provide another example, GPS (Global Positioning System) enables real-time delivery status and can also provide any additional data required. In the past, transportation of frozen or perishable goods was a risky business. However, GPS-enabled advanced solutions not only allow the company to monitor the real-time vehicle movements, but also allow checking the temperature of frozen goods inside a truck and issue instructions to the driver if required.

Apart from operational feasibility costs incurred in training or recruiting additional staff to run the solution as well as setting up infrastructure, a study of whether or not it is worthwhile to spend an X amount of time on the said project (schedule and time feasibility) is essential. For example, if something is going to be deployable only after five years hence, is it worth risking the unpredictable future of the solution?

A few other questions to be answered are:
- Does this solution conform to the existing culture within the organization?
- Is it likely to alter mindsets and, if yes, in what direction?
- Last but not the least, is the solution in sync with the laws of the land.

Returns on the investment, both tangible and intangible, will determine the value of the business solution.

2.5 Business Case

38. How do you define the Business Case?
A business case is the key document for obtaining approval for funding before starting a new venture. The work on the document begins once business needs, including problems and opportunities, are clearly identified and elaborated upon.

The business case document contains definitions of problems or opportunities, proposed solutions, timelines, and the budget required for the solution to be implemented, feasibility, risk vs. benefit analysis, cost vs. benefit analysis, and break-even or projected earnings/savings/benefits, etc. These are standard elements. There could be more items in the business case depending upon the novelty or project need. [Jane, 2015]

39. Who prepares the Business Case?
Stakeholder: At times, the stakeholder prepares the business case as he contributes actively in reviewing and validating solutions definition based on the business case and requirement documents.

Business Analyst: Actively writes the business case or facilitates a person working on it.

Project Manager: Facilitates writing of the document by providing data for calculating development and maintenance costs of the end-solution.

Finance Department: Actively participates in creating the business case when funding is from external sources. It is also involved in reviewing and validating the same to examine the feasibility of any new initiative before approving funds.

Business Owners: Proactively work on new initiative when funding is through external sources, such as a bank or investor(s).

Executive: A person seeking approval for internal or external funding for a new initiative.

Also, let's take a quick look at what matters and what doesn't while preparing a business case.

Purpose: Most importantly, understand the rationale behind your business case in order to remain focused while hard selling it. When you do that, it helps in presenting it to the management and convincing it to invest on new projects or initiatives.

40. What should the business analyst focus on in Business Case Analysis?

The following are the primary goals of analyzing the business case.
- Identify genuine stakeholders in order to obtain accurate data from to prepare the business case
- Never lose sight of your initiatives
- Check for feasibility
- Calculate and validate cost vs. benefit analysis
- Be prepared with supporting documents related to your previous projects in order to further consolidate you case.

More parameters can be added to the business case as per the requirements of the business as well as stakeholder data.

Thereinafter, it is over to the project manager, who provides total cost of the project and its ownership, including:

a. Development Cost:

- Maintenance cost, including technical support required to sustain the project that could either be outsourced or handled by an internal IT team;
- Hardware and software costs;
- Staffing costs, and
- Operational costs, which include the infrastructure for running a project.

b. Feasibility Check:
- Strategic fit for the organization in-line with its vision statement or overall organizational culture.
- Technical fit, and if not, how much additional cost it would entail.
- Financial fit in terms of being economically viable for the present organizational status. And if not, what options does the organization have within reach?

c. Cost vs. Benefit Analysis:

Cost

Tangible Costs
- Developing an existing project or working on new initiatives
- Employee training on a product or new initiative
- New user cost
- Hardware and infrastructure costs
- Software (operating system, security licenses, etc.)
- Relocation cost, as and when required
- Operational cost

Intangible Costs
- Disruption caused to any existing process vs. business while implementing a new solution.
- Recruitment and induction of new users.
- Any additional cost not covered here.

Benefits

Tangible
- Reduction in staffing costs
- Reduction in rental and operational costs
- Automation helps in improving quality by bringing down the possibility of human error and enhancing turnaround time.
- Reduction in inventory
- Reduction in miscellaneous costs

Intangible
- Enhancement in business image with improvement in quality of products and services offered.
- Increased customer satisfaction with better products and faster response.
- Rise in employee satisfaction with reduction of repetitive work.
- Better management of the information systems.
- Improvement in presentation.
- Better and faster corporate communication

d. Risk Analysis
- Identify risk based on previous success rate in similar projects or initiatives.
- Identify risk mitigation strategies.
- Explore all viable options before short-listing prospective vendors.
- Update cost vs. benefit as well as risk analysis documents throughout projects to mitigate risk.

Based on the above strategies, a business analyst or business owner can factor in ROI (Return on Investment), PV (Present Value), NPV (Net Present Value), FV (Future Value), NFV (Net Future Value) and breakeven point to support his business case.

In summary, the proposal must be factual, logical, doable and profitable. [Jane, 2015]

41. What is the Business Analysis Maturity Model?

Business analysis maturity model based studies conducted by BCS consist of two axes: the scope of work allocated to a business analyst and his level of authority. The scope may range depending on the initial study and role of the business analyst in exploring and defining the solution. Or, the authority of the business analyst may vary from limited (requirement analysis) to influencing and guiding senior company management (Business Process Re-engineering or Business Technology Optimization/Management). [Paul, Yeats et al. 2010]

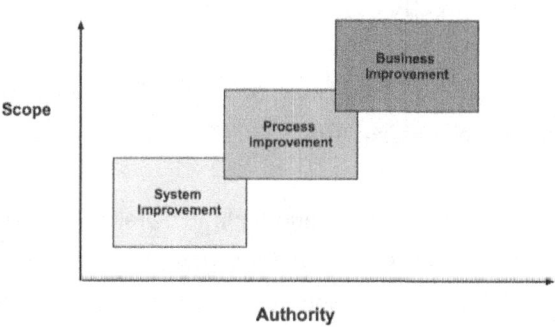

Business Maturity Model

2.6 Solution Scope

42. What is the System Boundary?

The system or solution boundary is an area that is alienated from features, functionalities, databases, or systems that will get altered (developed) and the items that will remain constant. It creates a particular scope for the future solution.

43. What is the System Context? What are the details and parameters required to define it?

System context defines the system environment that is relevant to a proposed system directly or indirectly.

The following characteristics of the system context may influence the outcome of a system/solution:

- People (business and technical stakeholders)
- Process (existing and future processes)
- Systems in operations that will be connected or communicated with the future solution
- Events (technical and physical)
- Reference documents (policies, operations, and regulations)

The following diagram shows the system elements in scope.

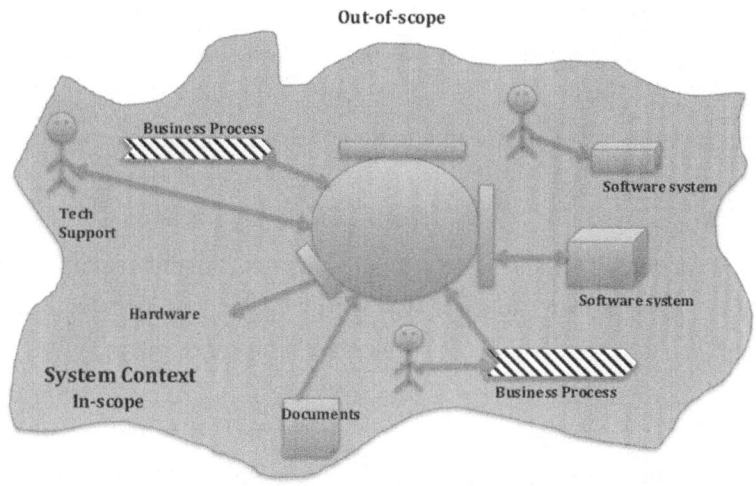

44. How do you plan for defining and delivering Business Change Strategy?

First, define the business idea or problem definition and required solution and organizational capability to implement the change. Solution capability will describe the high-level features and functionalities of the solution and non-functional requirements. The organizational capability will describe the resources, infrastructure, technology and other details required for operating the solution and making a smooth transition. Once the organization is capable of accepting the change, it should be implemented either in phases or in one go.

45. What is the Solution Scope?

The solution scope is the next level activity that the business analyst and project manager will work on together once the business needs are defined.

The purpose of defining the solution scope is to comprehend the volume and nature of work involved in the business solution-building model. It involves defining, designing, developing, deploying, and decommissioning the solution successfully, as also, assessing the impact of the new solution on the existing business, business processes, functionalities, and solutions. It means the solution scope will help in defining what will and will not be part of the "delivered solution". The same will be specified in terms of the solution capability and capacity. In addition, it also helps in identifying and addressing the existing challenges and capabilities in adapting the new solution.

At the end of the activity, the business analyst produces the solution scope documents, and other supporting documents such as list of stakeholders, list of capacity, list of capability, few high-level use case diagrams, data modelling, etc., which are relevant to the activity.

The scope model provides a realistic picture to the stakeholder to visualize the potential solution and its capabilities. The solution scope document also serves as the main basis for calculating budgets and scheduling stakeholders to understand the volume of work and intricacies associated in delivering the solution.

Furthermore, this also provides a guideline to business and IT teams throughout the project lifecycle and helps in avoiding scope creep. The scope document and supporting models will be the main sources to elicit and scope the requirements through the entire requirement management phase for finalizing the solution.

A well-defined solution scope provides a guideline to the entire team to remain focused on the solution and avoid possible delay or exceed the budget through use of scope creep.

If the solution scope is not defined correctly and completely, the team will encounter serious trouble in terms of realizing the solution successfully during its defining, designing, developing and deploying activities. The major issue will start while defining the solution, as there may be chances of it either going out of scope or resulting in inadequate requirements that ultimately lead to the completion of the solution within the stated budget and schedule, or in a worst-case scenario, unsuccessful delivery.

The followings are the basis of the initial solution scope:
- Business need
- High-level requirements (features and functionalities) of the solution (Use Cases)
- Additional input from subject matter experts (SMEs)
- Input and output data of the solution (data modelling)
- The nature of interaction with other systems (scope diagram)

46. How do you define the Solution Scope? What are the Business Analysis Techniques used to define them?

The following two methods support the solution scope document:

a. **Scope statement**
   i. Scope Model (amoeba-style free diagram)
   ii. Context Diagram or Data Flow Diagram
   iii. Data Modeling Diagram
   iv. High-Level Use Cases
   v. User Stories

b. **Alternative analysis**

a. Scope statement:

The scope statement can include details of the scope model, context diagram, data flow diagram, high-level use cases, and the user stories as applicable.

i. Scope Model: A scope model will have an undefined diagram resembling an amoeba, which depicts process, software, business rules, documents, hardware, etc., that are part of the solution scope.

ii. Context Diagram: A context diagram illustrates the solution or product as the core part sans details, as they are known only after requirement elicitation and analysis activities are completed, and external entities, such as other software solutions, hardware, network, document, process and so on are identified. These will interact with the solution. The interaction is part of the solution requirement, as this impact of external forces cannot be ignored.

Context Diagram

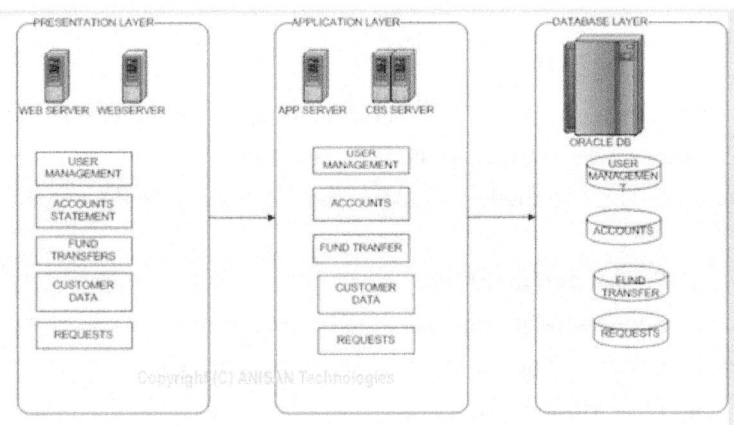

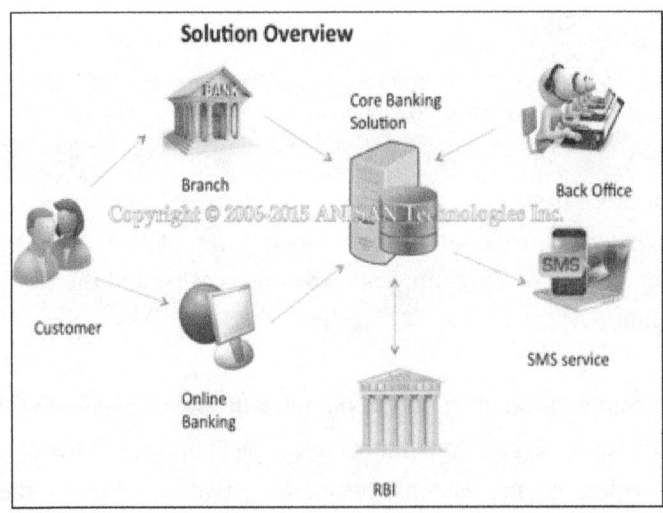

iii. Data Modelling Diagram: Data modelling (this describes the input/output data and logical modelling of database and system dependencies on other systems in terms of input and output)

iv. High-level Use Cases: Use cases (this describes people, their interactions, functionalities, dependencies, and communication with other systems in the environment that get integrated with new solutions)

v. User Stories: The user stories describe user requirements in concise and precise form. Please check the agile section for more details.

b. Alternative Analysis:
It is another useful technique that supports solution scope to evaluate the proposed solution through an analytical comparison of the operational effectiveness, cost, and risks of the proposed solutions to gaps and shortfalls in operational capability.

Additionally, the business analyst can use techniques, such as product roadmap or business requirement document, requirement analysis results, solution requirement (functional and non-functional requirements), and cost vs. benefit analysis to update the solution scope at a later stage.

47. What is Change Management?
A business analyst must also provide information about how changes in scope will be managed once the scope document is signed-off. It is obvious that the solution scope document will change whenever there is any feedback or review of either the business need or solution capabilities or the changes made to the delivery of any functionality to support their main features. During this phase, the business analyst must check if every requirement is in-line with the scope document and existing capability.

It is usual to come across such changes only after the solution is fully defined through the business requirement document (BRD), as this requirement document provides inter-dependencies of capabilities and their integration with existing system architecture or technology. Thus, incorporation of only a few changes will be mandatory after "business need" changes or functionalities are modified to align with the current system. A business analyst must keep relevant stakeholders informed before initiating any change.

The typical change management process will involve identification, definition, analysis (benefits vs. risk), proposition, suggestion, and recommendation.

A business analyst must update the scope documents along with the business need and other related documents. The business analyst must adhere to the change management process defined for the project to incorporate any changes in solution scope as it directly influences the entire solution in terms of schedule and budget. It may indirectly impact other solutions if it is not defined well and communicated to other system owners.

Please refer to the change management process for incorporating changes to the solution scope.

The solution scope model must describe:
- How people will interact with the business solution?
- What business solution will and will not be capable of high-level functionalities and processes mentioned in the business need?
- How the new system will interact with other existing solutions?
- What are the standards (based on both internal and external standards) the new business solution is required to follow?
- What is size of the business solution in terms of features, data, etc.?
- What are in-scope and out-scope items?

- What are the details of the business assumptions and constraints (both business and technical)?
- What are the details of the business need (a problem or an opportunity identified)?

The business analyst, with the help of major stakeholders and project managers will start defining the solution scope once the business needs are defined at a broad level.

The definition of scope lays the foundation of success for any business solution. The business analyst must be capable of getting the stakeholders to collaborate to get their inputs in a short span of time and conceptualize the solution.

The business analyst can use scope modelling, documentation, data flow and data modelling diagrams, use cases, interface analysis, and functional decomposition techniques to complete his tasks. The business analyst must have an adequate domain knowledge to elicit requirements and conceptualize the solution.

48. What are the key things to remember while defining the Solution Scope?

a. Identify Initial Stakeholders: To obtain correct inputs to guide one through defining of solution by providing additional domain knowledge and interdependencies of the solution in the existing scenario.

b. Manage Expectation: Able to manage the stakeholder expectations without allowing the scope creep.

c. Avoid Scope Creep: Able to restrict the scope using various options available. The business analyst needs to collaborate with business and technical team members for their guidance to explore various possible options to avoid the scope creep.

d. Self-Confidence: Able to convey the message to the stakeholder when there is any issue without getting emotional about any personal feedback that might be received.

e. Domain Knowledge: The business analyst must spend adequate time to understand the business environment or at least know who could be the stakeholder or SME to contact for validating requirements for the scope document.

f. Validation: Each document that the business analyst produces must be written, communicated, and validated through a formal process (sign-off process) before proceeding to the next phase.

g. Communication: The business analyst is required to communicate with the right stakeholder at the right time and also create an environment of trust to avoid any future conflict or confusion.

49. What is the content in the Vision Document?

The following is an example of structure of the vision document and it is followed by questions with detailed explanation of each item mentioned here.

Table of Contents
    i. Revision History

1. Business Requirements
2. Background
        2.1 Business Opportunity
        2.2 Business Objectives and Success Criteria
Customer or Market Needs
        Business Risks
Vision of the Solution
        Vision Statement
        Major Features
        Assumptions and Dependencies
Scope and Limitations
Scope of Initial Release
Scope of Subsequent Releases
Limitations and Exclusions
Business Context
Stakeholder Profiles
Project Priorities
Operating Environment

Revision History

Name	Date	Reason for Change	Version	Comments
<Person who made changes>	<Date changes are made>	<Provide description of the changes>	<Please provide the version after making the changes>	<Comments, if any>

50. What are Business Requirements?

Business requirements provide the foundation and the reference point for a detailed development of requirements. You may gather business requirements from internal and external stakeholders such as customers, management team, subject matter experts, department heads and project sponsors who have a clear idea of project vision and rationale. It is their job to justify the investment.

51. Describe project background.

This section summarizes the brief history of the new solution and need for implementing change.

Business Opportunity: Business opportunity describes the potential business opportunity after implementing the proposed solution. This potential solution can include new business lines, increased market share, increased brand value, etc. If the potential solution is replacing existing legacy systems, the opportunity will provide details of additional capabilities such as features, functionalities, improved technology, etc. In case the proposed solution incorporates new regulatory requirements, they need to be mentioned explicitly along with the risks of not implementing them. All these opportunities may be aligned with corporate strategy and goals.

52. What are the business objectives and the success criteria?

This section quantifies business objectives of the proposed business solution or business change. The success is measured in terms of direct and indirect benefits. These benefits are measured in terms of increase in revenue, savings in operational costs, improved customer satisfaction, etc. While specifying the benefits, it is also required to define the criteria of success through revenue projection for a certain number of years, return on investments, or increase in market share because of the solution to assess the final result. In addition to the benefits and success criteria, it is also important to review the feasibility, dependencies, and the risk factors of implementing the change.

53. Define Customer and/or Market Needs.

It describes the specific need of customers or market segments that will have to be met through a proposed business change. This will also describe why and how the current solution or capability is unable to handle current and future needs, thus, rationalizing the need for future solutions.

While defining a solution, it is vital to specify how the proposed solution, product, or change will impact customers in a positive way. How will the proposed solution work? What are the capabilities in terms of hardware and software a customer must possess to use the proposed solution efficiently? What is the level of security and performance criteria that the proposed solution will need? What features, or functionalities will the proposed solution require? These details are used in the future as points of reference.

54. Define Business Risks.

It is very crucial to define this along with the benefits and success criteria. The business risks can be in any form, such as market, competitors, user acceptance, new technology, negative feedback, unknown dependencies, or additional capabilities.

The team is required to identify these risks, address them and mitigate them effectively before successfully implementing business change.

There is a need to revisit these risks and update them periodically as a new risk may emerge or old risk may be required to be brought under control. These changes could happen at any time during the project lifecycle. Therefore, it is necessary to update the risk list and address them collectively. Another risk is not keeping the stakeholders informed, which may result in an understanding gap.

55. What is "vision" of solution?

Vision of the solution determines a long-term vision for the proposed business change and high-level overview of the solution and related systems required to implement change. It provides a high-level description of the solution context and major features or functionalities that the proposed solution will have. This vision document will be referred to throughout the project lifecycle to make decisions, understand context, validate scope, and plan project management activities.

56. Describe Vision Statement.

The vision statement can be a formal or informal document, depending on the novelty of the project and organizational standards. A formal document could be a structured description or a template to be filled out by the business analyst.

It is written in a succinct, clear, and crisp manner. It may include the purpose of the business solution and an end goal statement to achieve and impact the business solution upon implementation. The impact could be internal such as expected changes in terms of finance, technical, operations, resources, skill-sets, etc. The impact could also be external, such as market share, customer growth, and changes in the industry. The team must consider all the dependencies and other relevant factors to present them as realistically as possible. These dependencies and constraints could be the organization's capacity in terms of budget and human resources, skills set, adoption of new technology, etc. All these factors require validation against the organization's goals and objectives.

57. Describe the major features of solution.

The major features of a proposed product or system are explicitly mentioned, as these will be used to align and track the future requirements throughout the project lifecycle. They are bifurcated into the enhancement of existing features and the new additions. If new features are already available in the industry, the business analyst can specify the difference between the competitors' features and proposed features in the organization regarding the process, technology, usability, and any other benefits.

Any assumptions and dependencies are highlighted and formally presented to the stakeholders. A question could be as to what condition or capacity is needed in the organization or market to accept the new business change. This capacity can be a compatibility with the new technology, business process, and skill sets with an existing or a proposed future state. In addition, there are external capability factors such as supplier, client and customers' acceptability, and adaptability of proposed change without them making any significant investments.

For example, in the late 1990s, many eCommerce companies failed to take-off in India because the market, including the financial services sector as well as customers, were not comfortable with the idea of making online payments. They were okay with buying the goods but were not willing to share their credit or debit card information. Moreover, plastic currency wasn't very widely used.

58. Describe Scope and Constraints.

The solution scope will define what is included and what is excluded in the proposed solution. It will also consider constraints in the form of business processes, operations, technology or skill sets as specified. The solution scope is described explicitly and complemented with high-level use cases, data modelling diagrams, and system context diagrams. The business analyst presents the solution scope document to stakeholders. Any feedback received is incorporated as needed and presented again before obtaining an agreement and signing-off formally. The rigorous process of defining the solution scope will ensure that the relevant stakeholders are part of the discussion and that all other details are also considered. Any change in scope beyond this point is defined as passing through a well-thought-out pre-defined process that may impact budget and timeline of the project. The out-of-scope features will be either rejected or considered for future implementation.

The scope document may have more than one release during the project lifecycle. The initial release is based on the initial business need definition. The next release could be based on the outcome of requirement elicitation and analysis process or based on the solution approach or the revenue model analysis process. For example, if a vendor agrees to supply the proposed solution with additional features, those will be included in the solution scope at the time of signing of the contract.

There may be additional features, during the development or development transition requirement phase, when requirements and dependencies are further defined. These additional dependencies will be incorporated as required and will form a part of the subsequent solution scope release.

Out of Scope

Inversely, the proposed solution may not handle all the features mentioned in the scope due to various reasons such as budget, technology or employee skills set. Therefore, they can be further analyzed to either postpone or to reject them, depending on the condition.

59. What is the business context?

Business is a broad term and cannot be described by activities such as human resources, accounting, marketing, production, or line of products, such as clothing, car manufacturing, or industries, such as automobiles or telecom. These activities are done in a particular context. The context usually is dynamic and must be well understood. For example, recruitment can be described in context with an organizational goal, budget, skills set, future needs, location, local regulations, etc.

In business analysis, the context could be specific to an initiative, domain, strategic goal, customer need, industry standard, or global standard.

Therefore, the business analyst must understand business context from the perspective of a solution and organization's strategic goals.

For example, the business operation in context with eCommerce companies and retail chains may be different, even if they are part of the same industry. The business operations of a super luxury hotel and bed & breakfast hotel will be different due to different customer segments and their expectations.

These concepts are incorporated into the project in defining assumptions, constraints, priorities or everything. [Needle, 2010]

60. Describe the stakeholder profile.

The stakeholders can be defined as an individual, group, organization, industry, and government or regulatory body. Stakeholders can also be a category or group, depending on their domain, special needs, or user class.

They either influence the project or are affected by the outcome of business change. The stakeholders' involvement is based on the nature of initiative and stakeholders' role and responsibilities within the organization. For example, a recruitment manager who implements the recruitment processes will define requirements and problem areas along with current and future operating models. These models could be based on the user's daily involvement in the process. However, the human resources head may define or approve the recruitment policy considering future needs as well as overall organizational recruitment policy.

The stakeholders may have different perceptions and interests in the proposed solution based on their roles and responsibilities. These perceptions and interests are known as stakeholder values. The followings are a few examples of stakeholder values. These are both tangible and intangible.

- Increased revenue
- Increased customer satisfaction
- User-friendly application
- Reduced operational cost
- Standardized business process
- Incorporation of newly introduced regulatory requirements
- Reports for making effective decisions

The followings are the stakeholder values and associated details:

Stakeholder	Perceived Value	Needs	Interest Area	Constraints
Sales Manager	Increased revenue	Consider the solution to bring in 15% increase in market share.	The new unique features can be marketed to capture new customers and also brand the organization as a market leader.	Within 3 months.
Operation	Reduced	Reduced operating	Reduced resources and	15%

s Manager	operating cost	cost	overall operating cost.	reduction in operating cost.
Users	Easy to use	User-friendly and intuitive feature	Ability to locate and complete end-to-end operation with ease	Help document must be less than 1 page.

61. Describe the Project Priorities from different perspectives.

The business analyst prioritizes the requirements based on various factors such as schedule, features, quality, budget, etc., along with project objectives, constraints or limitations and degree of freedom available. The below table provides the examples of these factors in each category. The table provides balanced views.

Factor	Objectives	Constraint or Limitations	Degree of Freedom
Schedule	Release 2.0 to be available by 10/1, release 3.0 by 12/1	Release 1 and 3 must be completed by 12/31.	20 additional days as buffer.
Features	50% of high priority features will be in release 1.0		Min 40% high priority features must be included in release 1.0
Quality	The release must pass with 100% User Acceptance.	Since this is a regulatory project, no discrepancy allowed.	None
Staff	Maximum team size is 6 developers + 4 testers + 1 BA		Additional 1 developer can be added to expedite the work.
Cost	Within the budget	If cost is overrun by more than 18%, the work will be halted and resumed in the next financial year.	Over run up to 18% acceptable without executive review

Operating Environment:

These are details of the environment where the system will operate. These details are part of non-functional requirements and form the basis for defining the system architecture. They define performance, availability (time zone and operating time), failure recovery, hardware (details of hardware), and software (details of software it will be compatible with, for example, Excel and PDF compatibility for report generation), other technology or tool(s), interface, etc. Also, they may include the data source and format to communicate with the other systems.

For a detailed description of each of the above items, please check the non-functional requirement question.

Approval: List of names, designations, and signature of approving authority. They must be listed from senior to junior in descending order.

Reference: Please provide references used in creating these documents.

Glossary: List of terminologies used that are familiar to readers/stakeholder(s). [wsdot.wa.gov]

62. What is scope creep?

The term represents deviation of solution scope from what was originally defined, with or without impacting schedule and budget.

The reasons for scope creep are:
- Incomplete stakeholder analysis or identification of stakeholder
- Incomplete or incorrect solution context definition and scope document
- Poor communication and collaboration with business stakeholders and IT team
- Poor requirement elicitation, analysis, and review process
- Poor quality of documentation

- Lack of proper change management process for adding new requirements or modifying existing ones.
- Too much gold plating (adding too many new features or functionalities to the existing one)

63. How is scope creep avoided?

a. Context Diagram: Define the context diagram, verify and validate with key stakeholders and project management team to ensure that all external business and technical forces that impact the proposed solutions are well-documented.

b. Complex Project: Based on the complexity and related risks, the project manager can create a contingency plan in scheduling and budgeting.

c. Stakeholders Collaboration:
- Identify all relevant stakeholders and users in the initial stage and communicate goals and objectives of the proposed solution to stakeholders before eliciting requirements and setting expectations.
- Communicate scope, high-level features and deliverables to stakeholders using use case and/or data modelling diagrams.
- Collaborate with them during elicitation, analysis, and design phases.

d. Create a wish-list of features or product backlog of the proposed solution and prioritize them.

e. Define the change management process and communicate the same. This will help in setting expectations and lend seriousness to the process of changing requirements (if any) at the time of implementation.

f. Incorporate suggestions if they are relevant and necessary before commencing on the development work.

g. Document users' feedback on how they will interact with the proposed solution.

h. Continue with the development work only after the requirement documents are presented, verified, and validated; thereafter, stick to them.

i. Stakeholders can decide on additional requirements if the project is delivered within stipulated timelines and budget.

j. Lastly, it is the project manager or product owner that plays an important role in taking the initiative forward in a disciplined and focused manner, and rewards the team once it achieves the desired goal regarding project timelines and budget. [Carkenord, 2014]

64. How is solution scope validated?
Business Acceptance Testing (BAT) is one of business analysis techniques used to validate the solution scope. It is primarily focused on assessing business requirements of an organization and its strategy. It is based on approach, dynamics, culture, information technology, statutory requirements, operational framework, and customers' needs. It seeks to meet business requirements in a specified business scenario against the business case.

One can use solution assessment and validation tasks to validate a solution. If the solution(s) consists of more life cycles, the V-model can be used to map the business acceptance criteria with the relevant life cycle or iteration.

BAT is derived from business strategy or business requirements. It is directly related to an organization's mission, goals, and objectives. Such requirements are also known as business requirements (BR) at a higher level. The BAT may include solution covering automated requirements, usability, and manual processes. This could also involve ease of doing business or improving a process by reducing or altogether eliminating redundant and irrelevant steps/tasks in the process or adding the missing steps. This is also known as Fit for Business Testing (FFBT) and is conducted by business analysts working in that domain or department. It consists of key business requirements along with usability requirements, processes including auto as well as manual processes, business rules, etc.

The business analysts can use Strength, Weakness, Opportunity, Threats (SWOT) analysis or McKinsey's 7S Model or Balanced Score Card for analyzing and implementing such requirements. [Jane, 2015]

2.6 Assessing the Business Strategy

65. How is the business plan assessed?
A business plan is assessed on the following criteria:

Industry Dynamics and Analysis: What are the major challenges in the industry, and opportunities and risks associated with the product or services the new opportunity will face? Who are the major competitors and how can future products or services strategically positioned to effectively counter them?

Competitive Analysis: What are the organization's strengths and weaknesses?

Capacity Analysis: Does current capacity (business and technology) support new opportunities to create a competitive edge?

Strategy Analysis: What strategy will be used on a short-term and long-term basis? How will it justify the investment? What will be the return-on-investment (ROI)?

Risk Analysis: What are the possible risks and how can they be mitigated?

Business Plan Assessment Diagram

Industry Dynamics & Analysis
Competitive Analysis
Strategy Analysis (Short & Long Term)
Capacity Analysis
Financial Projection
Risk Analysis
Business Plan Assessment

66. How is project assessment completed?

The following are the criteria used to assess a project's success.

Vision

- Desire to resolve the business need (problem or opportunity)
- Business Need Document
- Business Case (Cost vs. Benefit Analysis)
- Sponsorship
- Governance and stakeholders' commitment
- Accountability: Roles and Responsibility

Solution Options

- IT (internal or external) capacity to execute
- Departmental or organizational willingness to accept the solution
- Ability to implement and operate

- Resource Planning
- Phase or Release Planning
- Risk Assessment and Mitigation

2.7 Strategy Analysis Techniques

67. What is "skill-analysis" matrix?

This matrix provides identification of competencies and business analysis processes to create a good fit between the two.

What

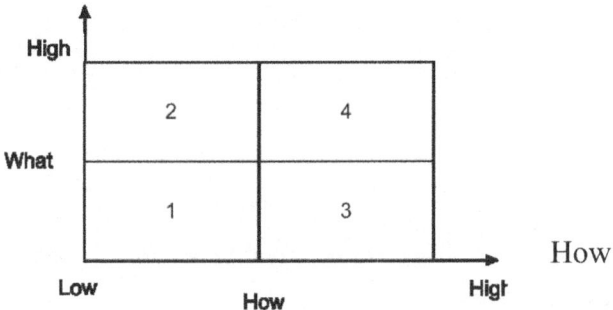

Skill Analysis Matrix

- First Quadrant:
- Understanding – "What" analysis is to be done and "How" it is to be done are not known?
- Second Quadrant:
- Understanding – Understand well "What" analysis is to be done, but "How" it is to be done is not known.
- Third Quadrant:
- Understanding: Understand well "How" analysis is done, but "What" analysis is done is not known.
- Fourth Quadrant:
- Understanding – Understand well both "What" and "How" analysis is to be done.

68. What is Porter's Five Force model?

This model is used to analyze competition that organizations face from business rivals.

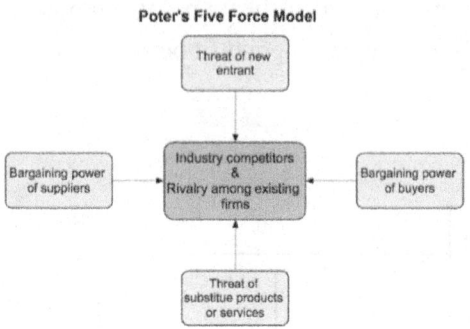

Based on the above diagram, the rivalry is defined from different perspectives as mentioned below.

- Threat from new entrants who offer substitute goods or services.
- Threat of substitute products and services: These include existing competitors offering similar products or services.
- Bargaining power of suppliers: The power of vendors that ensures smooth operations for producing and delivering goods and services to end customers. For example, coal supply to a thermal power plant is essential to generate electricity and supply it to the end customers. If there is any delay or increase in the cost of coal, that will have a direct impact on the business.

Bargaining power of buyers: The buyers' bargaining power will be high when substitute goods and services are readily available in the market. Inversely, it will be less if no substitute goods or services are available in the market. [Porter, 2008]

69. What is SWOT analysis?

SWOT analysis is analyzing Strength, Weakness, Opportunity, and Threats for planning strategy.

It is effectively used to analyze the current situation to define future strategy. In comparison with other analysis techniques, SWOT offers a long-term, integrated approach, including key company and environmental variables that may affect the future plans.

Internal Factors	Strength	Weakness
External Factors	Opportunity	Threats

You have control over internal factors in improving strengths and managing the weakness. What is needed is to analyze how these factors can be used in managing new opportunity and threats.
[Bohm, 2009] [Sarsby, 2014] [Pahl, Anne Richter 2009]

70. What is McKinsey's 7-S model?

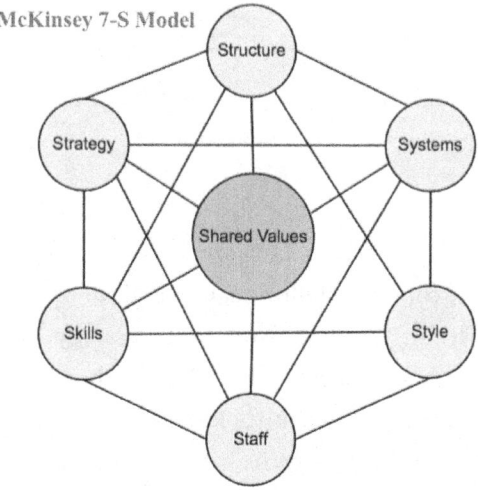

The McKinsey 7-S model considers that an organization is made up of seven interdependent components described as hard (Strategy,

Structure, and Style) skills and soft (Shared Values, Style, Staff, and Skills) skills.

The relationship is described in the diagram that shows the interdependencies of the components with one another.

If shared values get impacted, every other component also gets affected and changed as per the new set of values. The same is directly reflected in strategy, system, and staff, and indirectly reflected in structure, style, and skills. [Carroll, Walton 1997]

71. What is a Balanced Business Score Card?
This is a strategic balance of the organization.

Balance Business Score Card

[Diagram: Vision & Strategy in center, connected to Financial (top), Customer (left), Internal Business Process (right), and Learning & Growth (bottom)]

The diagram captures both financial and non-financial components of a strategy. It aligns the vision and strategy with decision and implementation management. It shows how the process of implementation works efficiently. Financial measure or investments reflect in other three perspectives, i.e., Internal Business Process, Learning and Growth, and Customers' need that are well-captured.

Many companies are using balanced score cards to elaborate and implement their strategic objectives. These can be done using the following model:

Objectives: We derive the objectives from vision and goal statements. Elaborate them in detail. For example, an organization wishes to improve customer service.

Measures: For instance, the measure could be to reduce customer complaints by 50%

Targets: Elaborate the target details. Within half a year, the organization will implement new customers.

Initiatives:
- Identify key issues in customer complaints
- Solution to resolve key issues
- Review post-implementation results
- Address exceptions

How can we link business perspective to the operational business decisions in a way that can be understood by business managers and then fully automate them?

First, create strategy maps and then model and link operational decisions to your strategic initiatives.

Optimize decision and process models. Link the results of each decision back to KPIs to create a self-improving feedback loop.

72. What is Pareto Analysis?
Pareto Analysis is a statistical, yet creative technique used in decision-making. It identifies causes of defects through statistical approach by organizing data into a logical order for better analysis, understanding and communication. The analyst uses the Pareto Principle or the "80/20

rule", which means focusing on 20% of work that generate 80% of benefits.

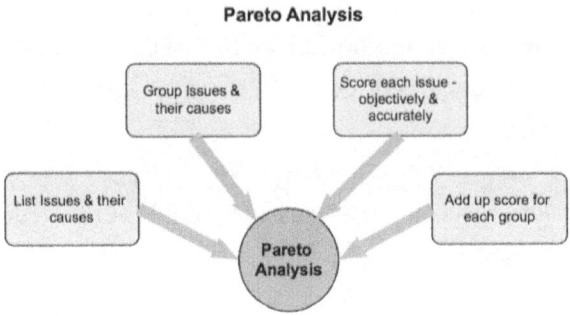

In project management, it is used in identifying issues that cause the highest number of defects. All the issues and related defects are placed in the graph. The issues causing maximum defects are identified and addressed first. [Kaliszewski, 2012]

73. What is Pair-Choice technique?
Pair-Choice is a technique that is used to prioritize various items in a single person or distinctive group setting. Each item is compared with every other item or paired with other items based on their importance or choice. The items could be requirements, values, or anything that may need to be prioritized. This approach helps to bring out objective analysis through prioritization.

	1	2	3	4	5	6	7	8	9
1		1	1	1	2	4	1	1	9
2			3	4	5	5	3	3	2
3				3	3	5	4	3	3
4					5	5	7	5	6
5						6	5	5	2
6							6	4	4
7								7	7
8									8
9									

The number of times an item is regarded as "the choice" is shown below.

Pairing, voting, and comparing the items in the table shows item 1 and 3 have five votes each, but item 1 is the winner as it has higher priority.

Item	Votes
1	5
2	1
3	5
4	1
5	4
6	2
7	3
8	1
9	1

74. Please explain the term "Force-Field Analysis"?

Force--Field Analysis is used in identifying supporting and opposing forces, and their intensity to affect the proposed solution.

Strengths of both supporting and opposing forces are analyzed to assess the impact of change. The result can facilitate timely intervention if the negative force is stronger and is likely to hinder implementation of the proposed solution in any manner. [Sabri, Gupta 2006]

Supporting Force			Opposing Force	
Strength	Forces for Change		Forces against change	Strength
5	Revenue through value added services	Progress Changes to Business System	Fear of new technology	3
3	Improved customer satisfaction		Learning additional skill	2
2	Improved Brand image		Confusion about future growth	1
Total = 10			Total = 6	

75. What do you know about 8-Omega?
It is a business change framework used for improving the existing business processes.

It addresses four dimensions or perspectives of business
a. Strategy
b. People
c. Process
d. Technology

As the name indicates, the framework has eight task types or, as a few may say, lifecycle phases within the grid and they are as mentioned below:

I. Discover
II. Analyze
III. Design
IV. Integrate
V. Implement
VI. VI.Manage
VII. Control
VIII. Improve

8-Omega Grid

	Strategy	People	Process	Technology
Discover		X		
Analyze			X	
Design				
Integrate				
Implement				
Manage				
Control				
Improve				

One to four recommended dimensions per cell of the grid can be paired with one of the eight tasks to complete specific project deliverable. For example, a discover/people grid cell (marked as "X" in the table) can identify stakeholders and their skills sets. In analysis or process a grid (marked as "X" in the table) can analyze requirements based on various requirement attributes such as priority, business value, cost etc.

The Omega-8 is a broad-based business change analysis model and is useful in specific context or coupled with other business change process modelling technique(s). [Graham, 2008]

76. What is FMEA? Where and how is it used?

"Failure Mode and Effects Analysis" (FEMA) is one of the techniques used to analyze failure, risk, and quality engineering. The technique involves reviewing components, systems and subsystems on various parameters such as functional, design, and process to identify failure models. The analysis result is used for risk holding and the mitigation process. [Stamatis, 2003]

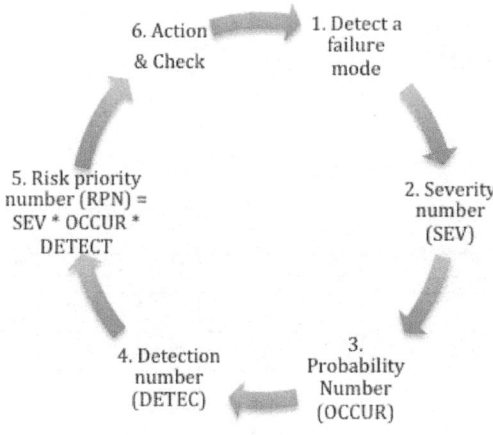

77. What is BCG Matrix? Or what is Boston Box?

This technique is used in strategy analysis. It is named after the management firm, The Boston Consulting Group (BCG), which developed it.

Strategy Analysis includes analyzing business units or product lines and allocating resources that are used as analytical tools in brand marketing, product management, strategic management, and portfolio analysis.

How it works –

The value of sales is denoted by a square for each product and service.

The growth share matrix provides a "map" of an organization's products and services, and its strength and weaknesses, i.e., current profitability and projected cash flows. The technique describes the main indicator points to the cash flow generation vs. cash usage that is aligned with market growth for a particular product or service. It provides a comparative study to make a decision for cash usage in a particular situation. [Griffin, 2007]

	Relative Market Share	
	Cash Generation	
	Low	High
Market Growth Rate / Cash Usage	**Question Marks** Earning: Low, unstable, growing Cash Flow: Negative Strategy: Invest, if it has potential otherwise well	**Stars** Earning: Low, stable, growing Cash Flow: Neutral Strategy: Invest for growth
	Dogs Earning: Low, unstable Cash Flow: Neutral or negative Strategy: Divest	**Cash Cows** Earning: High and stable Cash Flow: High and Stable Strategy: Invest to maintain current level or harvest
	Low	High

78. What is benchmarking?

The Benchmarking is measuring an organization's products, services, processes, performance, delivery, customer satisfaction, and so on against industry standards.

Xerox Corporation, the pioneer in implementing this technique, has defined it as, "The search for industry best practices which lead to superior performance."

Benchmarking is an ongoing process and can be measured against internal or external perspectives. The following are the three views.

- Internal (within the companies among divisions or department)
- External (within a company's external standards)
- Best Practices (best practices against best)

Author Sylvia Codling, in Best Practice Benchmarking: A Management Guide, observes, "Initially companies will practice with internal partners, progress to 'external' better practice partners and only gradually over a period of time build up to benchmarking against the 'best'." [Codling, 1992]

3 Project Management

The Solution Development Life Cycle consists of a series of activities starting from the phase of inception to disposition required to be carried out, depending on the project need. Please note that not all activities are suitable or required for every project. The following is the comprehensive description of the activities during each phase of the project life cycle.

Also note that the terminology that is used when phase changes occur is known as phase gate, exits, milestones or kill points. In case "the need" or "the business case" or "the return on investment (ROI)" on the project no longer justifies the investment due to various reasons, the destiny of the project may be decided during any of these stages. [Justice Dept., 2003]

3.1 Software Development Life Cycle

79. Describe the basic of software development life cycle.

Initiation Phase

The initiation phase of the project begins when a business need is identified regarding a problem or opportunity. Once the business analyst analyzes and defines the problem or opportunity, a project manager may be appointed to evaluate the feasibility of the solution. If the solution is identified as doable, the project manager will then present the estimate of cost and schedule of the new solution, based on its high-level requirements in terms of features and functionalities.

The initiation of a system (or a project) begins when the business need or opportunity is identified. A project manager is appointed to manage the project. This business need is documented in a concept proposal. After the concept proposal is approved, the system concept development phase begins.

Solution Concept Development Phase

When business needs are approved, the solution enters into the next phase to define and detail the solution scope. During this phase, the business analyst, project manager, and stakeholders define the boundaries and review the project for further viability and suitability.

This provides more insights into high-level features, volume of work, and time and budget required for realizing the solution in vision and scope document.

Once the rational and realistic solution scope, budget, and schedules are prepared, they are later presented to the sponsor to avail the approval for the solution. The business analyst, project manager, and stakeholders need to justify the investment in the solution by providing the detailed calculations on profitability and return on investment (ROI, payback period, break-even period, etc.)

Once the cost vs. benefit (Business Case) is found satisfactory, the sponsor may support solution development with or without any pre-conditions.

Planning Phase
Project planning starts once the project manager approves funding and solution in the form of a high-level solutions (business need and solution vision, and scope documents).

While the business analyst is busy in requirement analysis, the project manager works on resource management. It includes employees (with skills-sets) and plans for scaling-up timelines, IT resources (hardware, software, database, networking, communication channel, etc.), and other requirements to kick start solution development.

The project manager may need to check if any particular tool or specialized software is required for developing, testing, and deploying the solution. A detailed analysis is carried out for the legal requirements for managing data related to customers and defining the employee role with the help of the business analyst. Additionally, the project manager needs to check if any certificate and accreditation or vulnerability testing is required to validate the quality of the proposed solution.

The project manager will review the plan to ensure that the required capability is delivered on time and within budget. Towards that end, comprehensive project resources, schedules, activities, tools, and other data will be reviewed along with other technical team members.

Requirements Analysis Phase
In project management, the requirement analysis phase begins once the solution is completely defined, i.e., upon successful completion of documentation, presentation, scoping, verification, and validation of stakeholders' requirements. These requirements can be structured and documented in a formal template such as a business requirement

document (BRD) or a product roadmap. This template is represented as the solution definition. Furthermore, the defined solution is verified and validated against the organization's needs and capability before it enters into the requirement analysis phase.

At the requirement analysis phase, the business analyst prioritizes requirements on various criteria. After prioritization of requirements, each one is fully defined in terms of functional (functionality and features), non-functional (quality requirements such as system performance, security, reliability, and maintainability), and constraints and data specifications. The requirements are further modelled using various techniques for explaining it to reduce any ambiguity. These techniques could be process or activity diagrams, state diagrams, data modelling or class diagrams, entity relationship (E-R) diagrams, etc., as mentioned in the sections on business analysis techniques.

Once requirements are defined in detail as per the stakeholders (business and technical), the system design needs to proceed.

Each requirement must be verified against the basic criteria, i.e., to check if every requirement is measurable, testable, doable, consistent, correct, correlated, and concise to proceed. All these requirements are traced back to the original business need and solution scope to ensure that every requirement is in-line with the business need. If any requirement is found to be not related or out of scope, it is subjected to further analysis.

Design Phase
This phase is the "carrying out" stage, i.e., when the actual execution of the project starts. This phase begins only after the solution is defined through requirements and models, and verified and validated as viable, doable, profitable, and capable of being successfully deployed into the user community. If there is more than one solution option, each option is fully analyzed, ranked, and then selected.

Once the solution is defined, the project manager and team identify the physical characteristics of the system. These physical characteristics of the system and sub-system, along with the processes allocated to them, and their input and output are specified. Further, the detailed designs about the system and all related sub-systems along with their characteristics are used to create a detailed structure of the system. Each sub-system is partitioned into one or more design units, modules, or components for the purpose of development, with detailed logical specifications prepared for each solution module. Everything requiring user inputs and other related approvals must be recorded after completion of the process of due diligence.

The architectural diagrams are prepared, presented, and approved for the development work.

Development Phase
Once the sub-system and modules are identified and defined, the project release is planned based on requirements, priority, relevance, and resource availability. Sometimes stakeholders or business priorities are specified while planning for release.

The software is built in a series of releases, iterations, or modules. It simply means the solution is built through an incremental process (software coding, communication, and hardware), unit-by-unit.

Each of these units could be a small functionality, process, or piece of code. Each unit is systematically tested, integrated, and retested (regression testing) by the software engineer. Once the software is tested, it is assembled with hardware and retested for the entire module.

Integration
Once the execution level solution is built with one or more modules, those modules are integrated and retested successfully using regression testing before being shifted to testing or sand box environment.

If additional work is related to integration, the testing is required before transferring it into the sandbox environment; it must be completed at this stage. The integrated solution must be presented, verified, and validated by the technical team on business, technical, and quality-related criteria. The quality-related criteria such as software quality defined by the internal or external entities are checked.

Testing Phase
The testing team must ensure that the module is tested against the business, technical, and quality related criteria that are specified in functional requirement documents using various testing methods. Any bugs or issues that are identified must be reported, fixed and validated for quality thereafter.

The business analyst plans and conducts the user acceptance testing (UAT), and provides the results to the technical team. Therefore the technical team can continue to work if any requirement is either unworkable or not in-line with the requirements specified in functional requirement documents. Issues, fixes, and related results in UAT are verified and documented.

Once the testing team and users approve the solution, the system undergoes a certification and accreditation process.

Implementation Phase
Before deploying the solution into the user community (operations or production environment), the pre-deployment requirements (also known as transition requirements) are defined, developed and integrated with the solution.

The implementation phase continues until the solution settles down in the user community. During the settling-down phase, the reported bugs and issues are fixed, tested, and validated. This is to ensure delivering a better-quality solution and supporting a smooth operation in the future. Typically, it may take up to three months for the solution to settle down in the user community, depending on the solution and its complexity.

The implementation phase is complete once the solution becomes operational upon confirmation that it is fully functional and free of bugs, defects, or any other issues.

This may be referred to as the "closing" phase, and it is ensured that temporary activities related to the project are closed systematically. The business analyst, along with the project manager, completes the post-closeout project documentations. The stakeholders review these post-closeout documents and sign them off to formally close the project. These post-closeout documents are maintained in the project library for future reference.

Operations and Maintenance Phase
The operations and maintenance phases are monitored on an ongoing basis for its performance as mentioned in the business requirement documents.

The solution is enriched and enhanced to make it effective and efficient on a continuous basis so long as the solution stays in the user community or operations. These enhancements come from high-priority requirements categorized as out-of-scope or low-priority, with new changes being required to accommodate or replace due to an increase in capability to accommodate new situations or demands.

The change or new enhancement may enter into the planning phase, depending on the size, risk, and complexity of the initiative. Once it enters into the planning phase, it goes through every phase mentioned until it becomes operational i.e. completes the cycle.

The process of enrichment and enhancement continues as long as the system can adapt to the organization's need on a continuous basis.

Once the solution becomes obsolete due to an outdated technology or business, it can either be decommissioned or terminated in an orderly manner.

Decommissioning (Termination) Phase

Decommissioning implies the termination phase that is carried out in an orderly manner. It requires fulfilling organizational, local, and federal standards to preserve important data, information, and documentation. If required, the data retained can be easily retrieved and utilized in the future. Therefore, the data must be organized and structured for archiving. Proper planning for structuring, archiving, accessing, and documentation is required. The data is stored as per the organization's standards regarding information management systems, regulations, and policies.

The business analyst must perform a return on investment (ROI) again to validate the estimated business case against the original business case.

The ROI, business case validation and other data related to technical and business issues can be sent to a project library for archival under the "lessons learned" section for future reference. The data regarding unique issues or situations related to risk management, change management, and scope management also needs to be archived under the same category.
[US Department of Justice (2003) [Stellman, Greene, 2005].

3.2 Approaches

80. What are the different types of project management approaches?

Sequential: This is a formal project management approach. The project moves from one phase to the next, in a cascading effect, thus the name, "Waterfall" becomes apparent. Once initiated, the project cannot retract or skip this phase.

The entire project life cycle is formal, including requirement analysis, change management, designing, development, testing, and implementation. Other work related to project management, such as communication, change management, requirement traceability, and the approval process, is in the prescribed format.

Iterative or Iterative and Incremental: Iterative and Incremental development is one of the SDLC approaches used to produce software solutions through a series of demonstrable, executable releases of product/projects.

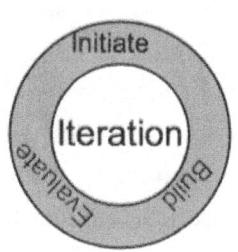

Every iteration can progressively contribute to developing and delivering a solution. For that, the team needs to plan, implement, and evaluate the solution in totality. Once the planning is complete, the team can organize the solution development into a continuous series of sequential or simultaneous iterations, depending on the comfort level and convenience of stakeholders, and complexity of the solution.

The solution/product is evolved incrementally, and the release usually consists of new iteration and enhancement/fixes (if any) of previous iterations based on feedback received.

These iterations are mini-projects and can be perceived as compact and self-contained projects. They undergo the entire software development lifecycle to produce a release of the project that meets the specified and agreed-on set of objectives.

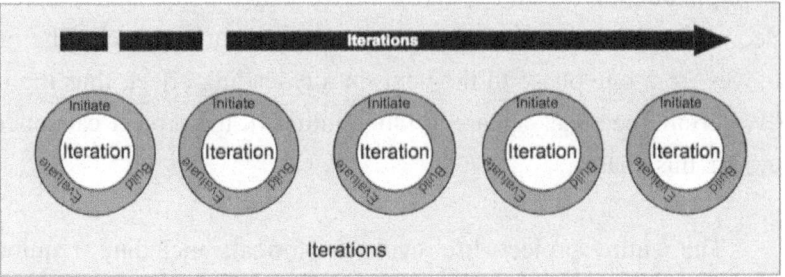

Iterations

Although the iteration is considered as a mini-project, different project dynamics are involved when it comes to dealing with milestones, resource management, interdependencies, and communication management. The project's progress is measured through the quality of each scenario built and tested.

Some of the standard features in iterative and incremental development approach are:

- Fast Paced and Frequent Delivery: Each release, iteration, or sprint consists of two to four weeks and is delivered in the form of workable components or features.
- Informal Communication: Informal communication involves close interaction among a small team of two to twelve members. Light and friendly communication and informal processes are followed. These meetings are frequent and face-to-face so that every team member understands the project's progress and outstanding issues, if any, can be resolved.
- Change Management: This is informal, with changes welcomed at a later stage.
- Customer Collaboration: Each iteration or sprint is delivered to the users to use. The end users provide the feedback or suggestions for improvements that are carried out at the time of next release.

- Informal Process: Every sprint or iteration is part of product or solution. At the end of the release of the component, the remaining components are assessed and prioritized for the next development. If any new requirement or component added is found to be important, it can be deployed before other requirements are developed, depending on its prioritization. Prioritization is part of every post-release (post-sprint release) activity, as there will be no changes added once the release or sprint is in process.
- Mini Project: From a technical perspective, each iteration is considered as a mini-project that goes through the entire life cycle phases (i.e., definition, requirement analysis, design, development, testing, and deployment) in a fast-paced manner.

81. What is the Hybrid approach?

Juyun Cho in his 2009 research paper, A Hybrid Software Development Method for Large-Scale Projects, recognizes that the conventional software development methods' potential to provide straightforward, methodical, and structured process in the software development. He further stated the shortcomings such as slow adaptability, impacts the project (budget and timeline) that leads to creating a negative impact on overall productivity. Agile complement the traditional methods in terms of shorter development cycle, higher customer satisfaction, lower bug rates, and quicker adaption to rapidly changing business requirements. But, agile brings its own shortcomings such as quality, stability, and security if sufficient testing, documentations, and systematic processes are lacking. [Cho, 2009]

The author further suggested that the hybrid model or approach can be used in combination with traditional and modern approaches, i.e., a combination of waterfall or Rational Unified Process (RUP) approach with an agile or spiral approach in building the solution. This is done purely based on the understanding and comfort level of the team. For example, RUP can be used along with the agile methodology to bring out the best of both approaches. In the research paper he concluded, "RUP is used as a skeleton in the hybrid method, while scrum is embedded into RUP to offer project management and tracking mechanisms through structure ceremonies, roles, and artifacts. It helps in mapping disciplines of both methods with each other." [Cho, 2009]

Castilla, another scholar, who referred to Cho's and other research papers, and suggested that RUP can be used as framework to understand the organization and to share the vision of core requirements. In addition, it can also support the activities, roles, artifacts, and disciplines during the initial stage. On the other hand, scrum can offer project management and tracking mechanism. The RUPs incremental and iterative approach allows incorporating the customer feedback in main documentation and focuses on the solution and the users' needs. [Castilla, 2014]

3.3 Agile

82. Please explain the "Agile" approach.

The agile approach is one of the approaches to the project management that is used in developing software solutions. It is a group of methodologies based on an incremental and iterative approach to help the team respond to the unpredictability of building a software solution. It also helps the team to explore the software solution as requirements continuously evolve through assessment and adoption, while producing the software solution through a series of demonstrable and executable releases of the product or project.

The process can be custom-made by developer, client, or organization, optionally based on the technical constraint, organizational standards, team's comfort, or project scope and budget.

Here, it is important to remember that each iteration progressively contributes to developing and delivering the solution.

The following are some of the "Agile" methodologies:
- Extreme Programming
- Scrum
- Lean Software Development (LSD)
- Feature Driven Development (FDD)
- Dynamic Systems Development Method (DSDM)
- Agile Unified Process (AUP)
- Adaptive Software Development (ASD)
- Kanban

Scrum is most commonly used as an agile approach in the modern information technology (IT) environment.

83. What is the Agile Manifesto?
- Individuals and interactions over processes and tools

- Working software over comprehensive documentation
- Customer collaboration over contract negotiation
- Responding to change in plans.

84. Explain Scrum or its usage of in a project?

Scrum can be used, as it is the most preferred agile methodology.

We can apply Scrum rules in managing and controlling iterative and incremental software solutions/projects.

The common strategies of agile are as follows:
- Iteration: Sprint are typically consisting of three to four weeks that are delivered in the form of a workable component or feature.
- Informal Communication: Since it is a close interaction among a small team (specify a number between two to twelve people).
- Light and Informal Communication: Along with informal communication, an informal process too can be followed. These are frequent and face-to-face meetings to understand work progress from all team members and resolve any outstanding issues.
- Change management: This is informal, with changes welcome at later stages.
- Customer collaboration: Each iteration or sprint is delivered to the user to access. The changes or improvement are done during the following release/s.
- Informal Process: Every sprint or iteration is part of the product or solution. With the release of a component, remaining components can be assessed and prioritized for the next development. If any new component is identified as important enough to be added, it can be accommodated before other complements are developed depending on prioritization. This is part of every post-release activity, with no changes added once Sprint is in process.

- Mini Project: From a technical perspective, every iteration or Sprint is considered as a mini-project that goes through entire life cycle phases (definition, requirement analysis, design, development, test and deployment) in a compressed and fast-paced mode. [Schwaber, Beedle, et al, 2002)

85. What is Product Backlog?

The "Product Backlog" is a prioritized backlog containing the end user requirements. It is also a prioritized list of the features (requirements or bug fixes, non-functional requirements, etc.) that covers a short description of all functionalities desired to be implemented to deliver the working or potentially shippable increments of the software product or solution.

It is used in place of traditional requirement specifications such as the Business Requirement Document (BRD) or a product roadmap or Software Requirement Specification (SRS).

The product owner owns the product backlog. The product owner and cross-functional team estimate and sign-off the delivery of potentially shippable increments.

Stakeholders and other team members can add stories/features/functionality/requirements to the product backlog in the form of a "To-Do" list.

The product backlog is enough to start work in Scrum instead of lengthy formal documentation used in the traditional project management approach.

#	User Story	Priority	Estimation
1	As an authorized user, I want to access 'manage beneficiary'	1	2

2	As an authorized user, I want to add a beneficiary	2	3
3	As an authorized user, I want to edit beneficiary	3	1
4	As an authorized user, I want to set transfer limit to the beneficiary	5	1
5	As an authorized user, I want to receive alter on my registered mobile phone after completing the transfer	6	2
	Total		9

- Each story adds value to a user or customer.
- Each story is prioritized and developed in order.
- Any team member can add or delete his story at any time during the project life cycle.
- However, a "sprint" or "iteration" can't be changed by adding or removing any story.
- The product backlog is analyzed and re-prioritized after every sprint, and based on the same, stories are selected for development for the next sprint.
- The product backlog is updated during the entire project life cycle.
- All stories are estimated.
- All the stories are complete within and no low-level tasks are added to the product backlog. [Schewaber, Beedle et el, 2016] [Jane, 2016]

86. Do you understand the term "an Epic" in an agile project?

There are many requirements scattered across multiple areas of the complex solution or product. The segregation and grouping of User Stories belonging to the same domain are known as "an Epic". An Epic is completed when all User Stories are added and concluded.

87. What is the "User Story" in agile?

A user story is a requirement or feature, or functionality described in the form of a story. The user story explains "who", "what", and "why" of a particular requirement.

For example, as an authorized user, I want to access "manage beneficiary" to add the new beneficiary.

This user story will define:
- Who - authorized user
- What - access "the manage beneficiary" functionality
- Why - to add the beneficiary

During the life cycle, these user stories are identified, prioritized, and selected for a sprint for implementing. They are further specified into tasks, estimations, and other details related to tasks.

88. What is Sprint?
Sprint is an iteration or a basic unit of the scrum approach. It typically consists of three to four weeks or 30 days. The software solution or software product is delivered through successive sprints.

89. What is a Sprint Backlog?
Similar to Product Backlog, a Sprint Backlog is a list of features and requirements that a team will achieve in the next Sprint. It is based on requirement priority and the developer team's ability to finish tasks.

90. What is the "Sprint-Planning" meeting?
The sprint meeting is conducted at the beginning of every sprint. The product owner, scrum master, and development team member(s) meet to understand the team's capability to create the "sprint backlog" by prioritizing items and planning and delegating work for the sprint. Although usually eight hours are stipulated for the meeting, it is difficult to fix duration for the same as the time taken to discuss and finalize the components may vary on a case-by-case basis.

91. What is "Daily Scrum" Meeting?

As the name indicates, these are meetings to define the short-term strategies. Every day during the sprint, the team assembles to discuss the progress of the sprint and strategy, if required. It is a short (average of 15 minutes long) informal interaction that can even be done at a team member's desk.

Each member answers three questions in turns:

1. What did I do since the last scrum meeting?
2. What do I plan on doing between now and the next Scrum meeting?
3. Do I have any roadblocks?

92. What is a Scrum (Kanban) Board? What is a "Story Board"?

This scrum board represents the progress in the agile approach.

You can create a virtual or a manual storyboard by placing a note on each section.

The columns indicate the stage and the row indicates the user story or task in a particular stage.

This is an excellent way to represent the status of the user stories or tasks along with the project.

Design	Development	QA Testing	UAT	Deployment	Done
Task L	Task H	Task E	Task C	Task B	Task A
Task M	Task I	Task F	Task D		
Task N	Task J	Task G			
Task O	Task K				
Task O					

Or

Product Backlog	In Sprint (Development)	Delivered
Task F	Task C	Task A
Task G	Task D	Task B
Task H	Task E	
Task I		

[Jane, 2016]

93. Explain the "Sprint Review" meeting.

At the end of the sprint or on the last day of the "sprint", there are two "sprint review" meetings – one for customer review and demonstrations and the other for the team to review possible improvements. Adequate time is allowed for the meeting and some can calculate it by deriving the value proportionate to the sprint time.

The duration of these meetings may vary. For each week of sprint duration, apply one hour of meeting time for the customer review. For the retrospective, apply .75 hours (45 minutes) for each week of sprint duration. For example, a 30-day sprint would result in a four-hour review and three-hour retrospective. A two-week sprint would result in a two-hour review and a one-and-a-half-hour retrospective. Additionally, the team should spend no more than one hour preparing for the review.

These are the meetings to review achievements and pending work.

94. What is a Sprint Retrospective Meeting?

Team members analyze past sprints to understand lessons learned from the previous project to avoid making similar mistakes and improve continuously.

95. What is Scrum Framework?

Scrum Framework outlines broad guidelines for Scrum projects with few rules (dos and don'ts), roles (Product Owner, Scrum Master, and Scrum

Team), artifacts (deliverables or prioritized backlog), and events (Scrum Planning Meeting, Scrum Meeting, Sprint Review Meeting, etc.) to deliver a software solution or products via iterative, interactive, and incremental approaches.

This framework provides the guideline for the role, nature of customer collaboration, communication.

It works on the principle of:
- Continuous Improvements: Inspect and adapt policy to engineering processes, products, and requirements.
- Change Management: An integral part of project life cycle.
- Thus, the framework allows defining only high-level requirements at the beginning and low-level requirements at a later stage or during implementation.
- Communication: The scrum product owner collaborates with the scrum master and scrum team to identify and prioritize user stories or functionalities.

96. Why do we use a Sprint Burn-Down Chart?
The sprint burn-down chart is a graphical presentation of the progress of the sprint that is required to know the progress of the overall project on a daily basis. It is updated daily during the sprint.

97. Explain the "Scrum Team" and its role?
The scrum team is comprised of the product owner, scrum master, and the development team.

Product Owner:
The product owner is a primary stakeholder of the software product or solution. He works intently with the team to create product backlog by identifying, adding, modifying, and prioritizing user stories.

Scrum Master:

The scrum master works as a facilitator in the project team. He manages resources, enforces scrum rules, leads scrum meetings, and guides the team as and when required.

Scrum Team:
The team decides what and how much they can do in a given project iteration or a Sprint. The team is responsible for developing and delivering the sprint.

98. What does Spike in Scrum mean?
Spikes are time-bound planned activities or sessions between Sprints created for analyzing or answering queries.

99. What is the Velocity of a Sprint?
It is the capability of the team to complete the work during a particular sprint that is derived from analyzing historical data.

100. What is a "Tracer Bullet"?
The "Tracer Bullet" is a spike or analyzing session using the latest technology, architecture and best practices in the industry to produce top quality products.

101. What do you know about "Impediment"?
Impediments are "the causes" that hinder a team or its member from achieving their goals or attaining to their maximum capability.

102. What do you mean by 'ScrumBag'?
The "ScrumBag" is the person or group or any factor responsible for 'Impediment'.

103. What do you know about "Invest" in Scrum?

"Invest" suggests the characteristics of a good "user story" based on the following criteria:

- Autonomous: No other "user story" is dependent on.
- Zero-Trade-Off: No further negotiation required.
- Value: The user story contributes sizable value to the end product.
- Scalability: The user story can fit various sizes quickly.
- Testability: It is testable to verify the success criteria of implementation of the User Story. [Scrum institute website, 2016] [Jane, 2016]

104. What is Planning Poker?

It is bringing consensus among the team on the estimation of a particular user story during the planning phase.

Planning poker cards are distributed to the team members. Each card has a number that is associated with estimations in the form of either hours or days. Once a user story is selected, every team member is asked to display their card that conveys their estimation for that user story. If all cards display the same number, that number (estimation) is finalized as "estimation" for the user story.

In case, cards display different numbers for a user story, estimations are discussed and finalized through consensus.

105. Provide important point to implement agile.

- To introduce the culture of supporting the fast-paced delivery model through higher flexibility.
- To train all stakeholders to understand the process and delivery model.
- To improve resource management

- To review the communication, risk and overall project management

106. What the difference between models?

	Traditional	Modern	Hybrid
Also Known as	Predictive, Predefined, Plan driven, Sequential	Dynamic, Iterative, change driven, adaptive	Combined, Fusion
Process	Pre-defined process	As-you-go	Overall project is pre-defined and each the iterations are as-you-go.
Formality	Formal	Informal	Either way or semi-formal
Communication	Formal meeting, templates and approval process.	Informal but written communication such as email, MOM or requirement matrices are fine.	Semi-formal, or formal or informal depending on the project size and preference
Requirements	Defined, Developed and Delivered in formally.	Defined, developed and delivered informally.	Defined and delivered formally, but developed informally.
Examples	Waterfall	Agile, Spiral	RUP

107. How do you define a project management approach?

The specific needs of each software solution depend on the business need, scope, complexity and stakeholders' comfort. The structured methods such as Sequential/Planned Driven (Waterfall) or Hybrid (fusion) or change-driven (Agile) will be suitable for a complex project that is well defined and has regular deliverables.

- Size of the project (number of stakeholders and technical resources)
- Impact of the project (number of business units impacted)
- Complexity of the project (number of unique requirements)
- Number of resources needed for the project

The plan-driven approach is suitable if the end goal is known and can be fully defined in the beginning. An exploratory or an agile approach is suitable if the end goal is not known (or cannot be identified) at an early stage. The technical team starts briskly working on the project at an early stage in an informal environment due to small team size and nature of the software solution.

4 Requirement Management Life Cycle

There are not more than five musical notes, yet the combinations of these five give rise to more melodies than can ever be heard. There are not more than five primary colors, yet in combination they produce more hues than can ever been seen. There are not more than five cardinal tastes, yet combinations of them yield more flavors than can ever be tasted.

— *Sun Tzu*

108. Describe the requirement management process.

The concept of requirements management applies to define all the activities that go into the planning, investigation, scoping, and defining the requirements of a new or altered software solution in the software engineering or business analysis. The requirement analysis is a vital part of the business analysis process, whereby business analysts examine elicited requirements as per the stipulated priority, establish relationships, and assign attributes to define them further. Requirement management is a part of managing requirements in terms of changes made during its lifecycle.

Alternatively, it is defined as "the set of activities that consists of gathering requirements, identifying the 'right' ones to satisfy, and documenting them." [Davis, 2013]

Requirement management helps business analysts identify needs of an organization as well as stakeholders. To achieve this, the business analyst needs to collaborate with the stakeholders to elicit requirements that can be defined as business and stakeholder requirements. After identifying these needs regarding requirements, these are further analyzed and scoped into a solution. [Stellman, Greene, 2005]

Requirements analysis is also known under other names:

- Requirement engineering
- Requirement gathering
- Requirement elicitation
- Operational concept documenting
- System analysis
- Requirement specification

Until recently, software engineering and requirement analysis were not perceived to be as significant as they are considered these days. The processes were mostly carried out either by a project coordinator or a project manager as extension of their role.

With increased complexity in defining the software solution and subsequently increase in cost of fixing the software solution or handling delays along with dissatisfaction of the requirements, the requirement engineering started to gain importance. This additional role was meant to reduce failures, delays, and mistakes in requirements and improve overall solution quality to meet stakeholder as well as organizational goals.

Given their importance, requirement elicitation and analysis are significantly demanding. It requires tremendous tact to collaborate with varied stakeholders. Besides, it requires a thorough understanding of business analysis coupled with strong domain knowledge to communicate with stakeholders effectively.

To understand the nature of the problem or business idea, a business need has to be defined. Defining the solution also requires additional knowledge about information technology to present the correct business solution that is:
- Feasible
- Doable
- Affordable
- Profitable
- Legal
- Ethical

While defining the business case, i.e., cost vs. benefit analysis, the business analyst will have to walk a tightrope to balance costs, consider risks, and present a realistic estimate of profitability. It requires him to have tremendous experience of business, technology, and the domain that he is working in. [Rowel and Alfeche, 1997] [Kotonya, Sommenville, 1998]

Requirement management consists of:

- Documenting requirements
- Tracking requirements
- Prioritizing requirements
- Managing changes in requirements
- Adding new requirements
- Removing unnecessary requirements
- Changing previously approved requirements
- Redirecting development staff
- Initiating a parallel development effort to satisfy new requirements
- Extending schedules
- Cancelling current efforts in part or entirely. [Davis, 2013]

109. What are the problems in managing the requirements?

The general difficulty encountered in requirement analysis is well defined:

a. The right people with adequate experience, technical expertise, and language skills may not be available to lead the requirement engineering activity;

b. Initial ideas about requirements are often incomplete, wildly optimistic, and firmly entrenched in minds of people leading the acquisition process; and

c. The difficulty faced in using complex tools and diverse methods associated with requirement gathering may negate the hoped-for benefits of a complete and detailed approach.

110. What are the user issues in managing requirements?

Steve McConnell, in his book Rapid Development, details a few ways users can inhibit requirement gathering:

- Users don't understand what they want.
- Users won't commit to a set of the written requirements.

- Users insist on new requirements after the cost and schedule have been fixed.
- Communication with the users is relatively slow.
- Users often do not participate in reviews or are incapable of doing so.
- Users are technically unsophisticated.
- Users don't understand the software development process.

[McConnel, 2001]

User requirements keep changing even after software development has started. At times, new requirements may sometimes mean changing the technology as well. So, it should be made very clear to the business users to know their objectives and expectation regarding the solution required beforehand (i.e., during SRS stage of SDLC), which is rarely the case.

Developer issues

However, developers are equally to blame. Typical problems caused by software developers are:
- Software developers and users speak different languages. Although there may not be issues between the business users and the technical team during the development phase, the problem arises when users experience the gap between expected and actual results. Since the technical team supplies or delivers the project, it is responsible for bridging the gap, if any, during the project development phase.
- Instead of developing the system to enable the users to achieve their goals, the software developers try to fit the requirement into an existing system.
- In addition to the above points, software developers are more focused on technical work and are often lacking in domain and communication skills that require them to effectively reach out to the users. [Baxter, Sommerville 2011]

The solution is to let the expert handle the role. Business analysis or requirement engineering is a specialized profile that creates a bridge between the business users and the technical team. The business analyst can develop harmony by communicating with the technical team as well as the business users in their language to bring them to the same level of understanding.

It is possible by describing requirements and complementing them with design (pictorial representations of requirements) that help in reducing the misperception and ambiguity if any.

The 1990s marked the emergence of several modern techniques such as Unified Modelling Language (UML), prototypes, and wireframes. Then, in the 2000s, many software tools were launched in the market for designing these diagrams. These designs aid in the requirement management lifecycle as well as the project lifecycle by reducing turnaround time and improving representation quality. These designs assist business users in validating and understanding their requirements before designing and developing a system.

These designs allow:
- Improvement in users' understanding
- Capture of user interaction
- Identification of alternate options
- Capture of process and business logic
- Capture of user inputs and data needs
- Identification of dependencies and other details

111. How do you define a requirement?
It is the capability (functionalities inherent in a solution) or conditions (quality criteria required by a solution) or any documentation that describes both the solution and achievement of an objective. It is also the constraint under which the proposed solution must function. [IEEE Std 830, 1998]

112. How do you define the design quality?

The following criteria are defined in designing the system [Badham et al., 2000]:
- The system should have interdependent parts.
- The system should adapt to and pursue goals in the external environments.
- The system should have an internal environment comprising separate but interdependent technical and social subsystems.
- The system should have equifinality. In other words, the systems goals can be achieved by more than one means. This implies that there are design choices to be made during system development.
- The system's performance relies on the joint optimization of the technical and social subsystems. Focusing on one of these systems to the exclusion of the other is likely to lead to degraded system performance and utility.

4.1 Elicitation Planning

113. How do you plan or prepare for elicitation?

We prepare the following things before conducting an elicitation session.

- Understand the business need and scope of the solution (if I am not involved in preparing it)
- Have strong domain knowledge and understanding of intricate details required for the elicitation.
- Identify stakeholders that are participating in the elicitation from the stakeholders' list.
- Select the most appropriate technique for elicitation.
- Inform the stakeholders about the elicitation session, their role, and elicitation technique to be used.
- Obtain confirmation from the stakeholders who are attending the session.
- Prepare for travel, stay, and other arrangements if stakeholders are travelling.
- Arrange conference room, meeting room, audio-visual equipment, white/smart board, papers, markers, and other things.
- Allocate enough time to complete the session.
- Arrange training, if required for the stakeholders participating in the session.
- Prepare supporting team members (moderator, scribe, and facilitator) for their roles.

In addition, we will do the following:

- If it is an interview technique, we obtain the consent for the time and meeting place. We also send a list of possible questions for the interview to all the participants, so that the interviewees come prepared for the session.
- If it is an observation session, we inform users and obtain their consent to observe their work or role.

- If it is a questionnaire, we prepare a list of questions for the participants and send it out.
- If it is "document analysis," we obtain the required documents.
- If it is a workshop, we make necessary arrangements such as conference room, audio-video equipment, white or smart board, etc. We send the invite and agenda well in advance for the stakeholders to prepare well. This preparation helps to reduce wastage of time preparing stakeholders on the day of meeting or during the meeting. If any stakeholder(s) has to travel to attend the session, we make necessary arrangements for the person's travel and accommodation etc. as a part of an additional preparation.
- If it is a use case or prototype, we prepare them for the walkthrough to the stakeholders to capture their feedback.
- If it is a mind-mapping or brainstorming session, we do not provide any background information to enable the stakeholders to think intuitively and provide their input(s).

114. How is requirement elicitation strategy defined?

The requirement strategy depends on:
a. Project type: It is an in-house or outsourced product that replaces existing solution by either adding a component to the existing solution or providing an altogether new solution.
b. Project size: It is a process change, implementing the local application, global project, and integrated solution. The project size also depends on the number of stakeholders, unique requirements, database size, business units, and locations.
c. Number of stakeholders involved: When more stakeholders are involved, a business analyst will have to plan how to accommodate their perspectives or requirements.
d. Type of requirements (using the Kano Model): Satisfier, dissatisfier or delighted. (Please refer to the Kano Model for more details)

e. Stakeholders' comfort: Stakeholders' convenience and comfort in using specific elicitation techniques
f. Business analysts' comfort: And lastly, a business analyst's comfort in handling domain, stakeholders, and elicitation techniques shortlisted by stakeholders.

In an interview, you can list all the elicitation techniques you have used in your last project. In addition, you can also list elicitation techniques deployed in the previous projects.

Most common elicitation techniques are interview, questionnaire, and survey, facilitated workshop, observations, document analysis, prototypes, use cases, mind map, and storyboard, or scenario building.

115. How can I get better at requirement elicitation as a business analyst without having any experience?

Requirement elicitation is not a standalone activity. It is comprehensive and requires detailed planning involving project approach, project size, stockholder details, organization standards, and managing resources and their expectations.

The actual elicitation is:
1. Preparing for elicitation
2. Selecting right elicitation technique(s) depending on the complexity of requirements, stakeholders' comfort, and business analyst's comfort.
3. Conducting elicitation
4. Documenting election results
5. Confirming them with relevant stakeholders
    a. Prioritizing requirements
    b. Organizing requirements
    c. Structuring requirements in a standard template
    d. Modelling requirements
    e. Verifying and validating requirements,

f. Managing requirements throughout the life cycle of the project and more.

You might like to check out this business analysis course (http://anisans.com/certificate-in-business-analysis.php) that teaches requirement elicitation using real life approaches.

116. What is a Kano model? How it is used?
OR
Describe main qualities of requirements.

This is a requirement categorization technique that categorizes requirements based on stakeholders' satisfaction level. It is used in the requirement elicitation process.

They are classified as below:

a. Dis-satisfier: Basic features and characteristics of the solution that must be provided to avoid dissatisfaction of users. These are subconscious requirements elicited through observation and document analysis techniques.

These constitute unspoken basic needs. For instance, on checking-in at a hotel, you expect to be attended to at the reception desk. If the receptionist is busy, you are politely asked to wait until one is available. However, if no one attends to you at the reception desk, you feel unwelcome.

b. Satisfier: There are standard requirements where satisfaction level is based on the level or degree of requirements. These are conscious requirements elicited through questionnaires and survey techniques.

These requirements are explicitly mentioned and are expected to be fulfilled. For example, if a receptionist recognizes you, greets you in a friendly manner and enquires after your day or offers you your regular preferred suite, you feel satisfied. This satisfaction is dependent on pace, preference, and priority of the service rendered.

c. Delighters: These are unexpected features or functionalities provided to make users happy. These are unconscious requirements elicited through brainstorming or mind mapping techniques. If a receptionist informs you that being a regular customer, the hotel is upgrading your room type with complimentary drinks and breakfast or an additional discount on the room, you are bound to feel delighted, as you weren't expecting it.

117. How is an elicitation session conducted? What process does the business analyst follows during elicitation?

It depends on the technique used during the session and stakeholders' comfort.

Although the business analyst follows the different processes for the different techniques, following are the most common practices:
- Record the requirement in the pre-defined requirement structure.
- Define the requirement relationship and dependencies with other requirements.
- Also note preliminary cost vs. benefit details for each requirement. This helps the team to easily validate requirements at a later stage.
- Obtain additional details about requirements (priority, business value, possible business or technical constraints and assumptions that are made along with their relevance to the existing business process/software solution/environment) are recorded.
- If the specific requirement needs additional follow-up, it is discussed (initial planning for people, data, and resources).
- For the purpose of an interview, some business analysts prefer taking someone along with them to take notes.

- For questionnaires, preferably send an email with the questionnaire or else create Web-based forms and send the link.
- Details are then captured and stored.
- As a part of the observation technique, the business analysts study the user roles and processes they handle to effectively understand what each person is doing.

4.2 Elicitation Process

118. What process do you follow from elicitation to defining the solution?
- Prepare for the elicitation by scheduling the elicitation session and plan well for all the required resources.
- Select the elicitation techniques and send it to the stakeholders if they are comfortable with it.
- Conduct the elicitation session. In addition to requirements, we define relationship among requirements and elicit the requirement attributes.
- Document and confirm elicitation results.
- Scope the requirements based on business needs and solution scope.
- Present requirements to concerned stakeholders and review them. After reviewing the requirements, we can structure and document* them for approval.
- (Document* - Here we created BRD or project baseline or product roadmap)
- Communicate the requirement document to concerned stakeholders.
- Re-visit the strategy analysis to verify, update and validate business need, solution scope, organization capability GAP details and business case to ensure that the defined solution suits the organization's needs.

119. How do you plan for managing your information?
A practical way of handling the project information is to create a checklist of documents required for the project. The checklist is then verified against the organization's project management office (PMO) standards.

Or

Obtain the standard project document list from PMO and customize it by adding the mandatory documentation items and optional documentation list.

As per the departmental or organizational preference, these documents can be saved in a common or shared drive by creating document folders, sub-folders or using tools such as JIRA or SharePoint, etc.

Access to the project information can be granted to some stakeholders based on their role within the organization and project.

A point to remember is that an edit or update option must be given to limited users to avoid untracked or unsolicited changes. One or two users, depending on the need, must be responsible for updating and distributing the document among relevant stakeholders. This will help in keeping every stakeholder updated with the latest changes.

120. How do you define the role of stakeholders in the project?

This is dependent on the role of a particular stakeholder in the organization and his interest in the project. The stakeholder analysis output document can be used to define the role of the stakeholders. Please refer to stakeholder analysis.

121. What are the problems that business analysts face during requirement elicitation?

a. Scheduling the meeting or workshop for stakeholders from different locations.
b. Availability of business stakeholders as they were busy with their daily routine and this was an additional task for them.
c. Incomplete or incorrect business case
d. Lack of clarity about solution scope
e. Constantly changing the requirements or scope creep
f. Delay in elicitation and approval

g. Conflict management while aligning the business requirements with solution scope

You can provide specific examples while ensuring that they adequately prove your ability to handle issues successfully.

122. What is JAD? Or what is a JAD session?

The acronym means "Joint Application Development" or "Joint Application Design" session.

It is a structured and facilitated workshop for all stakeholders from both business and technical sides to understand the design and development of the requirements. This involves a highly intense session to bring out the requirements and other related details, and validating them with the technical team.

Since the technical team and end users are directly involved in the session, this helps them in getting a better clarity on the requirements and the vision of the project.

It also helps to reduce errors that may have occurred due to lack of understanding.

Participants include facilitator, scribe, business analyst(s), end user, subject matter experts (SME), project manager, developer or tech lead, tester or test lead and database personnel.

The agenda, role, and communication details are provided well in advance for the team to prepare for the session.

- Facilitator: Moderates the session.
- Scribe: Takes down notes and details.

- Business Analyst: Drives the session through question and answers.
- Senior Stakeholder: Tiebreaker or final decision maker.
- Subject Matter Experts (SME): Provides guidance in his domain as necessary.
- End Users: Describe and confirm the requirement
- Technical Stakeholders (project manager or tech lead, database professional and implementation SME): They play a key role by understanding and providing technical guidance or support during requirements discussion.

123. How does business analysis help in resolving problems?

Business analysis helps in resolving a wide range of problems through business technology optimization and business technology management. The business side business analysis involves strategy analysis, i.e., process improvement, business change management, understanding the problem or opportunities, and providing the solution catering to the organization, stakeholders, and user objectives/needs. This may lead to improved customer satisfaction, internal processes, revenue, brand value, operational cost, reduce employee stress, help decrease time taken to deliver goods and services to customers and, ultimately, enable the organization to function better. The enhancement can either be restricted to isolated areas or be organization-wide. The business analyst supports the entire process as a catalyst so that business units or functions work without any disturbance from another function or business unit.

The business analyst's efforts can also result in fixing an existing function. If the business analyst or stakeholder comes across any area for an improvement in the existing solution that was earlier ignored or done in a wrong manner, the same can be fixed during requirement analysis.

A project manager's role is mostly related to developing and deploying the IT solution. However, the business analyst's role goes well beyond that to include the documentation of additional requirements and changes they come across during their work. Such additional enhancement may result into a new project, or reworking or extending the existing project. The business analyst also needs to work with stakeholders to monitor the process of implementation of business change that requires working with HR team to handle change in the roles and responsibilities, user training, perception building or consensus building among users.

124. What are the different types of requirements?
   a. Business Requirements
   b. Stakeholder Requirements
   c. Solution Requirements (Functional and Non-Functional/Quality Requirements)
   d. Transition/Implementation Requirements
   e. Constraints

Business Requirements: Business requirements are directly associated with business goals or objectives of the organization. Stakeholder requirements are associated with the business stakeholder and their interaction with the proposed solution. Both these requirements are captured through business requirement documents supported by use cases, activity diagrams, data modelling, and mind mapping diagrams

Solution Requirements: Solution requirements are defined as the capacity and conditions that the solution must fulfill in the form of functional, non-functional (quality) requirements, and constraints.

Functional Requirements: The functional requirement is the description of the capacity a solution must fulfill. These are described through features or functionality a solution must have. There are few functionalities having lower priority that can be defined as "nice-to-have". This will add value to the solution or enhance user experiences.

Non-functional Requirements: The non-functional requirements describe the condition that solution fulfills in terms of performance, safety, security, reliability, and so on.

Transition Requirements: Transition requirements are mostly defined and documented as part of the functional requirement document.

Constraints: These are either business or technical constraints in terms of process, business rules, regulatory needs, or technical limitations that a solution must comply with. [BABOK Guide v2 and v3] [Pohl and Rupp, 2011]

125. What is functional requirement and how it is elicited?

The description could be in a structured format consisting of unique ID of the requirement, name of the requirement, rationale of functionality, details of function, associated diagram, success criteria, assumption, constraints, priority, basic flow, alternate flow, exception, data requirements, and comments for an additional information.

The following is the sample functional requirement structure:

#	Items	Description
1	Req. ID	Unique # (234)
2	Requirement	Book a Ticket
3	Description	Customer should be able to book a ticket online using his/her credit card/debit card/PayPal
4	Success Criteria	Ticket booking and confirmation no.
5	Assumption	The user has computer, internet, and online payment option

6	Constraints	All servers (travel portal, payment gateway and airlines gateway) are working
7	Exception	Cancel or change the booking
8	Business Rule	Ticket can be booked from current date onwards till next six months
9	Model	Activity diagram (Ref. # 234)
10	Comment	Nil
11	Author	Operations manager
12	Owner	Operations Head
13	Use Case #	3456
14	Input data	One way or Round Trip, City, Date, Bus./Eco. class, select flight, payment confirmation
15	Output data	Confirmed ticket with number

Database requirements

At a high-level, the database requirements can be data modelling (Class Diagram or E-R Diagram), data mapping, data dictionary, etc., that could guide the team further. A detailed description is also provided in the section on business analysis know-how.

Other Requirements

Any additional requirements that are not specified elsewhere in the solution document (Functional Requirement Document - FRD or Software/System Requirement Specifications - SRS). These requirements could be legal requirements, international or country requirements, database requirements, reuse objectives for future solutions, etc.

Any other information or new quality criteria or section can be part of this section.

126. What are non-functional requirements? Explain them with an example.

Performance Requirements:

Specific performance conditions associated with functional requirements for various situations are stated here. These requirements are equipped with additional details regarding the rationale, process performance timings, and the number of users for an individual requirement or feature, and their intent of having them to make suitable technical design choices for the proposed solution.

For example, the number of customers able to transfer the funds online at any given point in time.

Safety Requirements:

These requirements are related to possible loss, damage or harm to the proposed solution, with details of actions taken into account to safeguard the solution.

These requirements include internal and external safety policy and regulations. If any safety certificate (such as the 'VeriSign' security certificate requirement for accepting payment online) will be obtained in future, safety requirements must be considered to satisfy the authorities.

Security Requirements:

Security requirements define the security and privacy requirements related to the proposed solution. They deal with the internal and the external threat of an unauthorized access to the solution. The role or user-based access details are provided as part of business requirement document or product roadmap and solution requirements (functional requirement document i.e., FRD).

Also, security certification details or any privacy laws applicable to the proposed solution are mentioned explicitly.

127. What are the software quality attributes?

Any additional quality criteria intrinsic to business or customers' needs and applicable to the proposed solution are clearly specified.

Some of the requirements are listed below:
- Adaptability: Is it adaptable in different environments?
- Availability: Is it available in specified business time or under mentioned schedules?
- Correctness: Are the data and calculation results correct?
- Flexibility (visual increase or decrease display information on the website): Is it flexible enough for the users? For example, is a visually impaired person able to increase or decrease the font size of the information displayed on the website?
- Website compatibility with many devices (browsers, mobile or apps): Is the application or website compatible with various browsers or on multiple Internet-enabled devices?
- Interoperability: The ability to operate on different operating systems.
- Maintainability: The ease or difficulty in maintaining the solution?
- Portability: The ability to port the solution from one machine to another.
- Reusability: The list of requirements or components that can be reused. More the reusability, better the return-on-investment (ROI).
- Robustness: Strength of the solution in withstanding extreme situations in a defined time period.

- Testability (testing parameters): Is the entire solution or part of the component testable?
- Usability (look and feel): Is it user-friendly? Do users need special training to use the solution or can they intuitively figure out its features and functionalities?
- Audit Trail: How are the unauthorized access details, i.e., audit trail captured? What are the parameters in the audit trail, for example, IP address, time of access, the time period of access, number of failed attempts, etc.?

The above requirements must have additional quantitative, testable, and verifiable details wherever possible. Additional attributes such as user preference, ease of use over ease of learning or display attributes can be specified.

128. What are the (external) Interface Requirements? Explain them in detail.

User Interfaces:

The user interface requirements are logical characteristics of each interface between a software solution and the users. These requirements may include sample screen images, Graphic User Interface (GUI) standards or company standards or parent solution or product standards for its components related to user screen layout, standard buttons, keyboard shortcuts, error messages, display standards, etc.

It is important to provide the details of a software solution component for which the user interface details are being documented.

Solution requirements (Functional Requirement Document (FRD) or Software/System Requirement Specifications (SRS)) contain the overview as there are separate documents created for the details for each component specified in the user interface.

Hardware Interfaces:

This explains the logical and physical characteristics of each interface between the proposed software solution and the hardware components of the system. These requirements include the hardware devices such as a printer, fax machine etc., their types (printer or their software versions), details of input/output data, and controlled interactions (commands) between the proposed software solution and hardware, and communication protocol requirements.

Software Interfaces:
This section explains the connection between the proposed software solution and other software systems or products (for instance, generating reports and saving them in MS-Word or MS-Excel or Acrobat for PDF version). This information includes the name, version databases, tools, libraries, incoming and outgoing data/messages, nature of communication, and/or application interface protocols. In addition, it also provides the details of how the data is shared in a specific way, i.e., data sharing mechanisms and constraints, if any. For example, if flight cancellation information has arrived from an airline, it must be disseminated to all those passengers booked on that flight.

Communication Interfaces:
This section explains the requirements associated with any communications functions required by a product, including email, network server, web-browser, electronic forms, etc. In addition to function(s), the communication format and standards such as FTP or HTTP or HTTPS (secured zone) are also described. It likewise includes the requirements related to communication security, encryption, data transfer rate, and additional synchronization mechanisms. Besides, it is also a standard format of email/SMS (text message) or any other communication along with the sample data that is in fixed and variable form. It must also explain the database details including table name, column attributes, data format, and a sample data. For example, in the case of a bank texting its customers about every fund transferred to or from their accounts the sample text message and format could be:

"Thank you for using ABC Bank Internet banking. Your Transaction Ref No IGABCDF5 for USD 220 on 06-Dec-16 07:30-ABCINB."

129. What are the key principles of user interface design?

Jakobe Nielsen defined ten general principles for user interface design. These principles are used industry-wide as a rule of thumb, and therefore, are known as "heuristics". These principles provide the guidance to the software developers as well as users how to evaluate the system. [Nielsen, 1995]

a. Visibility of system: The user should easily be able to view system status.
b. Match between system and real world: There must be a match between real world, i.e., user-specific language and logic.
c. User control and freedom: The users must have sufficient control and freedom while interacting with the system
d. Consistency and standards: The user interfaces must follow predefined consistency and standards throughout the system.
e. Prevention of errors: There should be emphasis on preventing errors.
f. Recognition rather than recall: The users should be able to recognize rather than recall the system.
g. Flexibility and efficiency of use: The system should assist flexibility and efficiency of use.
h. Aesthetic and minimalist design: The system should be aesthetic with minimalist design.
i. Help users to recognize, diagnose, and recover from errors. Error messages must be easy to understand and have suggestions to act on.
j. Help and documentation: The key document must be part of every system to make users self-reliant. This document should be searchable and well documented.

[Nielsen, Molich, 1990] [Nielsen, 1994]

130. How do you follow business rules in a project while working on it?

A business rule specifies the business or technical constraint as either "true or false". It defines business decision, business process flow or structure, the behavior of people or system, and subsequent actions under certain conditions.

For example, if a child below two years is traveling by flight, the ticket price is not charged, but the tax amount (as applicable) will be charged. When someone is booking a ticket and entering the details of the child being age less than two years old, the system will apply zero to the ticket price and only add the taxes to arrive at the total fare.

These business rules are documented during the requirement elicitation process or business process review. Gathering business rules for reviewing the processes from documentation or from source codes is termed as rules harvesting or business rules mining. The business rules are part of the main business requirement documents, functional requirement documents, or product roadmap either as a part of the requirement, specific section, or as part of the glossary.

Constraints: The business constraints or conditions mentioned in the requirement that needs to be fulfilled by the user or system to complete the work successfully. They prove to be a hindrance if the condition(s) are not met. These constraints or conditions are also known as the business rule. For example, a flyer can buy a ticket for 60 days (or less) in advance. It means the system does not support any flyer to book ticket 61 or more days in advance, due to this business rule.

In another example is - the system can't support any flyer to book a ticket from the current booking time to the next 30 minutes due to administrative constraints. This means that if a flyer is booking a ticket at 8.00 am, he/she will only be able to book on flights departing at 8.30 am or beyond.

Derivations:

Knowledge is transformed from one state or mode to another in the same or different form. For example, an airline passenger can use his PNR number to select his flight seat before departure. Or the total amount of the bill is used to calculate to derive the tax for the bill. [Adrian, 1990]

4.3 Requirement Management

131. How do you document requirements? Or what are the different types of requirement documents?

The requirement document is produced to communicate requirements effectively to stakeholders. This is used as a reference document for all project development work, such as designing a system, writing its code, building software, testing software, implementing a software solution, and training users. This document is also referred to for operation and maintenance of the system.

There are a set of requirement documents that are created, depending on the relevance and target audience. Some of the requirement documents are listed below.

Vision: A vision document may be alternatively known as a scope document. This is a high-level solution scope document that includes the context, high-level requirements in the form of features or functionalities, assumptions, constraints, benefits, and risks of the proposed solution. It also provides the project roadmap or development plan as per phases or iterations.

Terms of Reference (ToR): A ToR document may be created to bring all stakeholders to the same understanding and an agreeable platform. This provides a shared vision of the solution in one single document.

Business Process Description: It is an executive summary of an initiative. It describes the problem and the proposed solution in high-level terms.

Business Requirement Document (BRD): The BRD describes the behavior required of a software application. Its target audience is the customer.

Request for Proposal (RFP): An RFP is a document that may be distributed to parties outside the organization to serve as the foundation for contracting of IT solution development services.

Software Requirement Specifications (SRS): This describes the behavior and implementation of a software application. The target audience is the development team who will implement the solution.

An SRS includes a description of the problem domain, a decomposition of the problem domain, description of functional requirements, quality of service requirements, and assumptions and constraints affecting the proposed solution. It also includes requirement attributes and traceability information.

132. What are requirement attributes?

Requirement attributes comprise of any additional information about requirements. These attributes are used to analyze and prioritize requirements. They are also referred to while developing, testing and implementing requirements.

Requirements attributes could be:

Requirement ID: A unique ID assigned to the requirement for reference going forward.

Requirement Name: A short name (two to four words) for the requirement. For example, "Add Beneficiary".

Requirement Description: A short description of the requirement written in three to four lines.

Requirement Source: The person and department of the person who defined the requirement. Any ambiguity can be immediately referred to him.

Requirement Priority: It is assigned to the requirement based on its business value, dependency, and overall role within the organization. It could be quantified, categorized, or specified.

Requirement Status: This represents the status of the requirement, such as under review, approved, deferred, or rejected.

Requirement Risk: This represents the risk associated with the requirement. It can be quantified (0-5) or details can be specified.

Requirement Complexity: This describes the complexity of the requirement in analyzing, developing, and implementing.

133. How to manage requirements effectively?

The easiest ways include creating a requirement catalogue in Excel or storing requirement attributes in tools such as JIRA, Share Point, Rational, etc. The following is a sample requirement catalogue.

(The enlarged size picture is available on page number 276)

134. How do you manage requirement scope?

Requirement Scope management is done to establish and maintain requirement baseline and tracing of requirements, which are used for comparison. Requirement baseline becomes an internal agreement like a contract between a client and the project team. The list of requirements or a requirement catalogue is officially signed-off at the business requirement level, later structured in the form of a Business Requirement Document (BRD). The BRD can be called as the first official document available to all stakeholders. The base-lined list of requirements is further considered under change control management.

Structure Requirement for Traceability

Requirement traceability supports the ability to trace requirements throughout the system development lifecycle. It is an important technique that is used in detecting missing functionalities or identifying specific requirements not supporting the implemented functionality that has the following project benefits:
- Traceability supports in managing scope
- Traceability assists in analyzing impact of change
- Traceability helps in testing risk-based requirements
- Traceability allows users to link work products/requirements to their source(s)
- Traceability confirms that the requirement elicitation process is complete
- Traceability supports enhances overall quality
- Traceability facilitates controlling requirement changes

135. What is a Traceability Matrix?

The Traceability Matrix means a matrix to trace information, or data, or documents. In business analysis, it consists of a table that correlates the requirements and maps their relationships. It can be in the form of parent–child–grandchild or mathematical relationship such as cover, subset, etc. For example, business requirements vs. functional and non-functional requirements or functional requirements vs. use cases or use cases vs. test cases. In addition, it can be used to trace high-level design to detailed level or features to requirements

To make it effective, the relationships must be defined in traceability matrices, including backward and forward traceability to ensure that the changes are easily tracked against the source and the impact on other dependent requirements.

The high-level requirement features are mentioned as column attributes. Detailed requirements derived from respective requirements can be listed in rows, as given below, or as recorded. The null value (empty) cell having no relationships exists with the requirements mentioned in the column head. If it gets too complex while creating a many-to-many relationship or 3D or 4D tables, you can simplify it further. Please refer the table below.

Requirement Traceability											
ANISAN Bank Ltd. - Online Banking Solution											
Requirement Traceability Matrix											
Business Requirement (BR) No	Functional Activity	Requirement Description	Prototype			Development			Testing		
			1.1	1.2	1.3	1.1	1.2	1.3	1.1	1.2	1.3
BR - 001	Activation	Activation of online Banking Facility	X			X			X		
BR - 002	System Security	Password Management	X			X			X		
BR - 003	View	Customer should be provided the functionality of viewing online SOT as well as download the same		X			X			X	
BR - 004	Transact	Online Transfer of Funds		X			X			X	
BR - 005	Transact	Registration of Beneficiary account		X			X			X	
BR - 006	Transact	RBI Batch upload			X			X			X
BR - 007	Alert	Text Message alert for transaction			X			X			X

A Traceability Matrix is used to:
a. Trace requirements

b. Establish a relationship with other requirements using various relationship definitions
c. It also establishes relationships with data or documents
d. Trace work products with the source
e. Track progress of requirement development
f. Reduce the risk of missing requirements
g. Identify requirements that are unlinked and may be a fit case for elimination if they are not serving any useful purpose.
h. Support in analyzing the impact of change on other related requirements.
i. Help the team to understand the requirement in totality.
j. Support in improving overall quality.

136. How do you prioritize Requirements?

Requirements can be prioritized using just a matrix and assigning the requirement attributes to them. In a complex situation, they can be prioritized by using prioritization techniques such as 6-hat, score-card, MoSCoW or Time Boxing techniques.

Please refer to the prioritization technique mentioned in the strategy analysis section

137. What is a 100-point method?

It is a prioritization method that is used to prioritize the items or requirements in a group.

Each member of the group gets 100 points and is asked to assign them to items based on their perception of its significance. The items that garner the highest points are accorded high-priority and can be listed in descending order based on their score to be later segregated into medium or low-priority.

For example, the table on the next page captures the requirement prioritization through a ranking process. Each stakeholder is given 100 points to assign it to the requirements listed under the requirements column. Care should be taken not to exceed the point 100 or leave any points in the bucket. The assignment of the score is entirely up to individual discretion, the perception towards specific requirement, and the preference of a requirement.

We have highlighted Martha's score as she has randomly assigned 10 points to each requirement. This means that either she has not understood or is simply not interested in participating in the prioritization process.

Chris and Rahul seem to be close buddies or both exercise great influences on each other as their score is the exactly same for each requirement.

At the end of the exercise, the business analyst adds the score for each requirement mentioned in the "Total" column and ranks them based on the score each requirement has received. For example, requirement 1 got the maximum score (76), so it is assigned as priority number 1, while requirement 8 got the least score (27), so it is assigned as the last priority, i.e., 10.

#	Requirements	Chris	pradeep	Martha	Prashant	Rahul	Total	Ranking
1	user login + Profile Management	18	10	10	18	20	76	1
2	Fund transfer	12	20	10	12	20	74	2
3	Bank Statement	10	20	10	10	9	59	3
4	Bill Payment	15	5	10	15	10	55	5
5	Customer Requests (order check book + stop payment)	10	20	10	10	7	57	4
6	Credit Card	5	5	10	5	8	33	8
7	Loan Application	10	10	10	10	7	47	6
8	Overdraft Facility	5	0	10	5	7	27	10
9	Tax filing	10	5	10	10	6	41	7
10	FAQ	5	5	10	5	6	31	9
		100	100	100	100	100		

138. What is MoSCoW?

- MoSCoW are requirement prioritization techniques, with requirements categorized as under:
- Mo – Must-to-Have (Must be implemented as they are specified in the document)
- S – Should-Have (The requirement must be implemented, but are there alternate ways of doing it.)
- Co – Could Have or nice to have (If schedule and budget permit)
- W – Won't Have (For this release, will be considered in future)

REQUIREMENT ID	BRIEF DESCRIPTION	CRITICALITY (MoSCoW)
FR-001	User registration is mandatory	M
FR-002	Change password	M
FR-003	Reset password	M
FR-004	Security question	S
FR-005	Security verification	S
FR-006	Alternate email	Co
FR-007	Notification on change in user's IP address	W

139. What is Time-Boxing?

Time-boxing is a requirement prioritization technique that helps stakeholders and business analysts to categorize requirement into high, medium, or low-priority. This comes in handy in projects with a fixed budget or schedule, where stakeholders add the best requirements from the requirement bag (all-out) or remove the worst (low-priority requirement) from the requirement bag (all-in), leaving high-to-medium priority requirement until they attain their target (budget/schedule).

Illustration: In the following table, there are ten requirements that are prioritized as high, medium, and low during requirement elicitation, with the technical team having provided the estimate of developing each requirement in terms of time and cost. A business analyst needs to coordinate with stakeholders to select them based on priority, budget, and time. This is useful in a fixed cost or timeline project.

#	Requirements	Priority	Time (in days)	Cost (in USD)
1	a	High	2	200
2	b	Med	5	500
3	c	Low	4	400
4	d	Low	1	100
5	e	Med	2	200
6	f	High	5	500
7	g	High	7	700
8	h	Med	9	900
9	i	Low	8	800
10	j	Med	3	300

For simplifying the cost calculation, we have derived the cost by the multiplying the number of days with USD 100.

All-In: All requirements are in the hypothetical box. The worst requirements (lowest priority requirements) are removed until we reach our goal in terms of time and cost. So, we removed the requirements c, d, i, h, and b, depending on their priority, cost, and time.

All-Out: This is the exact opposite of All-In. All requirements are outside. We add the best (highest priority requirement first) in a hypothetical box until we reach our goal in terms of time and cost. We have added requirements a, f, g, b, e, and j in order of priority, cost and time.

Voting: Stakeholders vote for requirements, and requirements with highest votes are considered high priority requirements for the proposed solution. This can be similar to 100-point score.

Selective: Stakeholders select requirements based on their preference, need, role, and responsibility.

Fixed Budget and Fixed Schedule:
Fixed Budget: Please refer to the new table on the next page. Hypothetically, if we have a fixed budget of USD 100,000 allocated for the project, we can select all high-priority requirements first and one medium priority to adjust the budget to attain to our target i.e. Req. # 1, 2, 3, 5, and 4. Please refer the table on the next page. (We have taken all high-priority requirements and added medium until we reach our budget)

Fixed Schedule: This is similar to fixed budget, except we have fixed time instead of fixed budget. For example, if fixed schedule = 120 days, we can select all high priority requirements first and add medium priority till we reach our budget. (Requirements. # 1,2,3,5,4, and 7)

Requirement Prioritization (Time boxing)						
#	Requirements	Priority	Time	Cost	Fixed Budget	Fixed Timeline
1	User Login + Profile Management	H	15	15,000.00	15,000.00	15
2	Fund Transfer	H	20	20,000.00	20,000.00	20
3	Bank Statement	H	25	25,000.00	25,000.00	25
4	Bill Payment	M	12	12,000.00	12,000.00	12
5	Customer Request*	H	25	25,000.00	25,000.00	25
6	Credit Card Application	L	42	42,000.00	-	-
7	Loan Application	M	22	22,000.00	-	22
8	Overdraft Facility	L	35	35,000.00	-	-
9	Tax Filing	M	20	20,000.00	-	-
10	FAQ	L	35	35,000.00	-	-
			251	251,000.00	97,000.00	119
* Order check book + Stop payment)						
Fixed Budget: Hypothetically, if you have a fixed budget of USD 100,000, you can select all high priority requirements first and 1 medium priority to adjust the budget to reach to your target i.e. Req. # 1, 2, 3, 5 +4						USD 97000

Fixed Schedule: Hypothetically, if your fixed schedule is 120 days, you can select all high priority requirements first and add medium priority requirements till you reach your timeline i.e. Require. # 1, 2, 3. 5. 4 & 7	119 days

140. How do the business analyst and team work on developing a product from an idea?

- By performing market analysis, competitor analysis, strategic vision, and feature sets the team can outline the future solution (To-Be).
- By performing a SWOT analysis, feasibility analysis, and capability analysis the team can understand the current capability (As-Is).
- Gap analysis, related capability requirement, and scope analysis will help to understand what is needed to make the transition from an idea to a product.
- The future product is tested through feasibility analysis, business case (cost vs. benefit) or ROI (return on investment) to understand the feasibility and profitability of the product.
- Requirement elicitation will define the product, its features, and functionalities, while requirement analysis will prioritize its requirements or features.
- The product is developed, integrated and tested through the project management process before it is ready for transitioning into the user community.
- Scalability is done through the production, packaging, and distribution process.
- Packaging, shipping, and distribution (if it is on CD or any other form of hardware) are completed.
- Alternatively, it is uploaded and integrated with proper security and payment process on a website so that it will be ready for customers to pay and download the software product.
- The product is enhanced and enriched through user feedback and the experience captured in various ways. These updates are distributed free-of-cost (not charged) or charged depending on the novelty of the upgrade and value it offers to the customers.

141. What method or standards do you follow to document the elicitation results (not defining the business solution)?

We use templates to document every requirement. We ensure that requirements are written in natural language.

For instance, at an initial stage, it was a simple matrix that captured all the requirement attributes. Additionally, we created process diagrams, use cases, class diagrams and other models wherever necessary to support the requirement.

142. What are the standard elements in a business requirement document?

Table of Contents
- Document Information
  - Revision History
  - Document Approval History
  - Introduction
  - Product/Solution Scope:
  - References
  - Business User of the Solutions (Stakeholder list)
  - Definition and Acronyms
  - Business Requirements
  - Reporting Requirements
  - Design Constraints
  - Appendix
  - Glossary

Document Information
- Current Version: The current version of the document.
- Owner: The name of the owner of the document.
- Date Last Updated: The date it was last updated
- Last Updated By: The name of the person who updated the document.

- Author: The person who needs to be contacted if there is any clarification needed on the document.
- Date Created: The date the document was created.
- Approved By: The name and designation of the person who approved the document.
- Approval Date: The date the document was approved or signed off

Revision History:

Version Number	Date	Author	Brief Description of Changes	Comments

Document Approval History:
- Role: The role of the approving authority
- Name: The name of the approving authority
- Signature: The signature of approving authority
- Date: The date of approval obtained

Introduction:
- Description of User Problem/Project Background
- Business Need (Project Scope)
- [Project Scope of the Project Charter.]

Production/Solution Scope:
- Briefly explain the boundaries of the proposed solution and the environment in which it is supposed to operate.
- Clarifying the scope and limitations to establish realistic stakeholder expectations. Sometimes customers request features that are too expensive or do not fall within the intended software solution scope.
- High-level features (Including customer requested features)
- Alternative features details are required if the cost of the feature or the functionality is too high. These details are inclusive of pros and cons of alternate features.

- Environment (operating environment + any web browser)
- What is not part of the scope? The list of out-of-scope items.

References:
- List all documents that serve as inputs to the Business Requirements Document. These could be, but not limited to:
  - Policy documents
  - Regulations
  - Minutes of the meeting (MOM)
  - Project library
  - Official communication
  - Books or other sources
  - Additional link or source would be convenient for stakeholders to verify their doubts against source information.

Business Users of the Solution (Stakeholder List):
- Please refer the stakeholder analysis description document to list the potential business users of the software solution and their details.
- For each category of user, provide the requisite information.
- Business Users and roles of the To-Be system will be revisited for definition while defining workflows.

Definitions and Acronyms
- The definitions and acronyms section describes unique words, terminology, symbols, and notions used in the documents that may be specific to the department, organization or industry. The definition supports the readers from other domain to understand the entire document and also reduces the chances of multiple interpretations, if any.

- The author defines all the terms as required to interpret the specific document, including acronyms and abbreviations. Also, includes the definitions for terms that have multiple usage or unique company usages.

Alternatively, a centralized glossary for the project would help in reducing the redundant work.

Business Services and Processes:
- List all the major services and processes used in the requirement documents. The services or processes in that list can be described along with the process or activity diagram. This will reduce the chances of multiple interpretations.
- **Business Rules:**
  Any business rules that can apply to a particular requirement or can apply to the entire solution are stated here. For example, a business rule in a travel portal is to apply a 30% discount if the traveller books the hotel room along with the flight ticket. This business rule is particular to the requirement. However, the business rule that disallows cancellation of a highly discounted ticket and hotel room, is implemented in the entire solution.

Business Requirements

Simply put, the business requirements are high-level descriptions that are associated with the business goals and objectives. Business requirements identify the benefits of the proposed solution to the organization and its customers. The vision document or "Terms of Reference" are referred to in developing the requirement document.

Business requirements are listed as major features that are needed to satisfy the stated goals, objectives, and strategies for the project.

There could be an additional template to structure the requirement. It may include following elements:

Requirement ID		Requirement Type		Use Case #	
Description					
Rationale					
Source		Source Document			
Acceptance/ Success Criteria					
Global/Local (Select One)		Specify Input/output			
Priority		Urgency			
Status		Complexity			
Change History					

- Requirement ID: Unique number associated with the requirement.
- Requirement: 2-4 words describing the name of the requirement
- Type: The type of requirement such as business requirement, stakeholder requirement, functional requirement, non-functional requirement, or data requirement etc.
- Use Case #: Use case number associated with this requirement. If it is not available, we can add it at a later stage.
- Description of Process: Brief description of the process or any other model that can complement the requirement description.
- Rationale: Justification of requirement
- Source: Source of the requirement, usually the department or division where the requirement originates.
- Source Documents: Any document from where the requirement is generated.
- Acceptance/Success: What is an acceptance or success criterion of the requirement.

- Global/Local: Requirement is global or local in nature.
- Input/Output: Input and output data needed to implement this requirement
- Priority: Describe the priority of the requirement either as "high", "medium" or "low", or quantify "0-5", where "5" is the highest.
- Urgency: Describe the urgency of implementing the requirement either as "high", "medium" or "low", or quantify "0-5", where "5" is the highest.
- Status: Describe the status of the requirement as approved, not approved or under review.
- Complexity: Describe the complexity of implementing the requirement either as "high", "medium" or "low", or quantify "0-5", where "5" is the highest.
- Change History: A brief description of the change history of the requirement.

Reporting Requirement:

- List of reports and their details needed by stakeholders.

Assumption and Constraints:

Assumptions and Other Relevant Facts
- This includes any assumptions made for the business solution, and its systems and requirements during the analysis or decision-making phase.
- It may also consist of relevant details of internal as well as external factors that may impact the proposed solution.
- Most business requirements are to be met by the Corporate COTS (commercial off-the-shelf) tool of choice. If there are any that are not met by the tool, they shall be not implemented in the system.
- All other assumptions are listed in the Project Charter and Project Plan.

- Assumptions:
- The list of all the assumptions made for the solution that was considered to be true.
- For instance, the customer will make an online transfer. The customer has online banking access details.

Constraints:
- Business Constraints: Only authorized customer having a valid user ID and password can make an online transfer.
- Technical Constraints: If the beneficiary's or centralized bank's server is down, the user cannot complete the transfer.
- If the user has changed his mobile number and not updated the same, the transfer can't happen, as the user will not get the security code to validate the transaction.

<u>Design Constraints:</u>
- Any unique conditions, internal or external that may limit the requirement or software solution in part or fully constitutes design constraints.
- There are two types of constraints - design constraints and project constraints. Design constraints are documented here. If any project constraints or dependencies related to business rules that impact requirements are identified, document them under project constraints. Other project constraints and dependencies that are related to budget, cost, and schedule shall be updated in the project plan or project log, respectively.

<u>Appendix A – Glossary</u>
- List of the terms, abbreviations, definitions, and relevant information used in this document or in software life cycle.
- Additional Details: The elements in this template will depend on the software solution requirements and can be customized as needed.

143. Explain the difference between assumptions and constraints.
<u>Assumptions:</u>

Assumptions are future scenarios that are considered to be true, but they are not verified. For example, before launching Amazon Inc., Jeff Bezos made an assumption that people would buy books online, which was not the norm back in those days. His hunch turned out to be true and his venture became successful. If this assumption were proved wrong, the venture would have been unsuccessful and there would be no Amazon today.

Constraints:
Both business constraints and technical constraints are the current limitations imposed on the software solution that may impact on its development and design, as they are mandatory requirements to be considered.

For instance, talking about business constraints, the online payments need to be integrated to existing payment gateways.

Under technical constraints, the payment process shall adhere to existing and 'VeriSign' certification requirements related encryption, data format, and other requirements.

144. **What are the main reasons behind business analysts missing requirements?**
     - Incomplete list of stakeholders (or stakeholders are not identified) and their requirements are missed.
     - Incomplete or incorrect analysis of current state (As-Is) that will have an impact on quality of future state (To-Be) as the requirements that need to be carried in proposed solution will be missed.
     - Incomplete or incorrect solution scope will lead to incomplete list of requirements. These are mostly interface related requirements that may have a serious impact on the proposed solution in terms of timelines and budget.

- Lack of trustworthiness that might be impacting effective communication and collaboration with stakeholders and team, creating a hindrance in getting a better insight into the proposed solution. This may lead to the business analyst missing out on crucial requirements or business rules.
- Lack of adequate domain knowledge of business analysis may impact on the requirement elicitation, analysis, documentation, and management processes. The business analyst may not be able to ask the correct questions or may not know if the requirements are incomplete or incorrect in case other team members miss this part.
- Lack of traceability in which the requirements may potentially result in a poor-quality solution. If the requirements are not traced using proper traceability matrix or other similar measures, you may miss the requirement during requirement development and the change management processes.

145. What is requirement analysis?

Requirement analysis includes examination of requirements across prioritizing, structuring, specifying, modelling, documenting, verifying the quality of requirements, and validating the system requirements against the business solution as well as the organization's needs. They may also be known as software requirement specifications (SRS) or functional requirement documents (FRD). In addition to Functional Requirements, FRD also includes business as well as technical constraints and non-Functional Requirements (non-FR), i.e., quality or capacity related requirements of the proposed solution.

146. What is the process of requirement analysis?

Requirements are prioritized and structured using standard templates (functional requirement document (FRD), software requirement specification (SRS)) with verified and validated descriptions, models, matrices, etc.

The prioritization is completed using various techniques, such as JAD session, MoSCoW, Score Card, and voting. During or after prioritization, members of the technical team participate in the meeting to discuss the requirement feasibility and constraints (business as well as technical).

The prioritized requirements are structured, modelled, and documented in a template (functional requirement document) that is later verified and validated.

Once the document is reviewed and signed-off, requirement analysis process is considered as complete. However, this process is repeated each time there is a change in the existing requirement or a new requirement is added.

147. When do you finish with requirement elicitation?
- All requirements are elicited from the concerned the stakeholders mentioned in stakeholder analysis and elicitation process.
- All requirements are verified for their completeness, clarity, consistency, and configurability (modified and confirmed), and the same are validated against business need and business case following stakeholder approval.
- All requirements are presented, reviewed, and approved by concerned stakeholders.
- All requirements are documented and the document is signed-off
- All requirements are prioritized.
- After completion of the above activities, the requirements are part of the solution scope and planned for release based on their priority.

148. Why do we use configuration management and version control system?

As defined by Anne Mette Jonassen Hass in Configuration Management Principles and Practice, "Configuration management is unique identification, controlled storage, change control, and status reporting of selected intermediate work products, product components, and product during the life of a system."

Configuration management is for maintaining the same design, materials, composition, or processes, or any other relevant factor specified in the original vision of the system through its entire lifecycle. [Sorrentino, 2016].

From software project management perspective, it includes software, hardware, tests, documentation, version control of project documentation or deliverables, release management, etc. It also includes an organization building a product or software solution, releasing it and tracking the changes. [Berczuk, Appleton, 2004]

Any alterations required to the existing system are also incorporated and documented in the original specification. These updated documents or designs shall be distributed to all relevant stakeholders, including users, for them to refer to for operation and disaster management. [Sorrentino, 2016]

149. What is the process of versioning (tracking) the requirements?

The requirements evolve and change during the project lifecycle. This happens as the project progresses. It is due to a better understanding of the requirement, its scope, and its relationship with other requirements, its constraint, and its impact as we progress during the project lifecycle.

It is important that the history of every version of requirements is maintained to understand how it has changed over a period of time, why it was changed, and at what point it has changed.

Revision History

Version Number	Date Updated	Revision Author	Brief Description of Changes
1.0	Mar, 01, 2012	Robert Smith and Ajay Rao (BA)	Initial Draft
2.0	May 5th, 2012	Robert Smith and Ajay Rao (BA)	Stakeholders feedback incorporated
2.5	Sept 23rd, 2012	Robert Smith and Ajay Rao (BA)	Added Security validation requirement to provide secured online fund transfer facility to the customer

This simple matrix will help the keep a track of the requirement document history. The versions are depicted with number and increment is depicted with decimals. For instance, in a "2.5" version, "2" is the version and "5" is increment. The version gets revised when a major change takes place and increment is revised when minor change takes place.

150. What is a software requirements specification (SRS) document?

Until recently, software developers elicited the software requirements and structured them into a single requirement document. That was referred as a software requirement specification document (SRS) and was used as one of the project deliverables. The future work was based on the software requirement specification (SRS) document. The SRS document included functional as well as non-functional requirements. In 1998, the Institute of Electrical and Electronics (IEEE) defined the software engineering standards for writing SRS documents known as IEEE std. 830-1998. [Rocha, Correia, et al. 2014]

The software solution requirements specification document consists of functional requirements, non-functional requirements, and constraints that are part of the requirement analysis phase.

Functional Requirements

They define the internal functioning of a software solution. These include calculations, technical details, data manipulation and processing, and other specific functionalities that show how the use cases are to be satisfied.

Data Requirements: These include structural and static-structural data. The static-structural data consists of inputs and outputs of the systems. The static-structural data consists of data usage and dependency of other systems. (Pohl and Rupp, 2011)

Behavioral Requirement: Information of the system and how it is embedded into the system based on business rules, user roles, particular cases, and other criteria. These are elicited through requirement elicitation sessions from users, stakeholders, subject matter experts, etc. [Pohl, Rupp, 2011]

Non-functional Requirements

Non-functional requirements are the system constraints or conditions needed for the system to function, and they are referred to while designing, implementing, or operating the system. They can be performance requirements, quality standards, design constraints security, etc.

Non-functional requirements can be adjectives that describe characteristics of the system in part or full. For example, the system should be reliable, i.e., it should be running 24/7 on 365 days with .001 margin of acceptable errors.

The functional requirements are outlined after defining business requirement and aligning these business requirements with business need and business capability. Models such as use cases, process diagrams or activity diagrams, class diagrams, etc., are made to support the functional requirements.

(Please refer to functional requirement questions for more details.)

Software requirements must be clear, correct, unambiguous, specific, and verifiable. [Rocha, Correia 2014]

151. How to manage the Requirement Scope?

Requirement Scope management is done to establish and maintain requirements baseline and tracing requirements. These are used for comparison. Requirement baseline becomes an internal agreement like a contract between the client and the project team. List of requirements is officially signed-off at the business requirement level, in the form of the business requirement document (BRD). The BRD can be called as the first official document available to all the stakeholders. The requirements outside of the base-lined list of requirements are considered under change control management.

Structure Requirements for Traceability:

Requirement traceability supports the ability to trace requirements through the software development lifecycle. It is an important technique to detect or identify the missing functionality if the implemented functionality is not supported by a specific requirement. It has the following project benefits:
- Traceability aids scope management
- Traceability aids change impact analysis
- Traceability aids risk-based testing
- Traceability helps linking the work products to their source
- Traceability supports in confirming that requirement elicitation process is complete
- Traceability supports in increasing the overall quality
- Traceability facilitates requirement change control process

152. What is a Requirements Traceability Matrix?

Requirement traceability matrix helps in tracing back to original requirements. For example, you may have created a set of features. Through the requirement traceability matrix, you can trace the features back to the original requirements. It is very rare to have a one-to-one mapping of features to requirements. Usually, several features will map to one requirement. The requirements traceability matrix is useful to show stakeholders that what they will deliver is directly linked to addressing the requirements and, eventually with the business needs.

A traceability matrix is a table that correlates any two base-lined documents that require a "many-to-many" relationship to determine completeness of the linkage. It is often used with high-level requirements (sometimes known as marketing requirements) and detailed requirements of the software product to the matching parts of a high-level design, detailed design, test plans, and test cases.

Requirement Traceability									
ANISAN Bank Ltd. - Online Banking Solution									
Requirement Traceability Matrix									
Business Requirement (BR) No	Functional Activity	Requirement Description	Prototype			Development			Testing		
			1.1	1.2	1.3	1.1	1.2	1.3	1.1	1.2	1.3
BR - 001	Activation	Activation of online Banking Facility	X			X			X		
BR - 002	System Security	Password Management	X			X			X		
BR - 003	View	Customer should be provided the functionality of viewing online SOT as well as download the same		X			X			X	
BR - 004	Transact	Online Transfer of Funds	X			X			X		
BR - 005	Transact	Registration of Beneficiary account	X			X			X		
BR - 006	Transact	RBI Batch upload			X			X			X
BR - 007	Alert	Text Message alert for transaction			X			X			X

Requirement traceability is convenient to establish the relationship among the requirements using various relationship definitions. This information is useful to understand the impact analysis if the requirement is changed and also to help the team to understand the requirement in totality.

The numbers of relationships are added up for each row and each column. This value indicates mapping of the two items. The null (no value) values indicate lack of relationships. It must be determined if one must be made. Large values in the column imply that the relationship is too complex and should be simplified.

Identify Scope Change Resulting from Requirement Change:

Scope changes stem from the following types of requirement change:
- New
- Modifications to existing requirements
- Removal of requirements already in-scope

As per the organization's change control policy, a formal change control process is used to identify, evaluate, trace, and report the proposed and the approved changes to requirements. Depending upon the level of requirement change, it may either not impact managing the requirement not-at-all, or it may slightly or drastically change the requirement, which will have an impact on the project scope, time, cost, and the overall quality.

If and when the requirement has changed, the business analyst determines the impact by updating the requirements traceability matrix in preparation for the approval or negotiation process.

The business analyst determines if the requirement-change is aligned with the objectives of the project. If it is not, then the business analyst starts the organization change control process to obtain the approval and sign-off or exclude and deem it out of the scope of the project.

The business analyst reviews and compares the requirement change with existing requirements with all key stakeholders and determines its relative priority and business value. He also determines any gaps due to the requirement-change and takes steps to have the gaps fulfilled.

Once the approval process is complete, the requirements traceability matrix is updated and it becomes the new baseline to which requirement changes are compared.

153. How do you select solution?

If you are buying a software package, you can consider following criteria to evaluate and select the right one for your requirement. This is similarly applicable while selecting an IT vendor to build and implement customized software solutions for an organization.

Request for Proposal: It requires sending out enquiries to software package companies or IT services provider companies that specialize in this domain. The request for proposal will include details such as business needs, data requirements, regulatory requirements, if applicable, and other relevant details. These details are essential for the suppliers to understand the potential product and specific customization or intricacies in building the customized solution.

Proposal Evaluation: Consider all the relevant factors, such as does the software package or solution meet the business goals in terms of business needs, features, functionalities, data, reports, capability, etc. The proposal will have details of software packages, features, developer profile, training and help documentation details, and support options.

Quality Evaluation: The business analyst can evaluate the software package quality with respect to internal quality criteria and industry standards, if applicable. In addition to this, there will be specific measurements such as a required set of functionalities, technical response, data requirements, lead-time, security, etc.

Vendor Evaluation: It is important to evaluate a potential vendor to understand their capability, specialty, customer response, reputation, and ability to support the solution in future.

Cost Benefit Analysis: Cost vs. Benefit analysis is the most important part of the process to convince the sponsor on benefits of the proposed investment. This analysis will have the total cost of the solution as well as the operating cost against the tangible and non-tangible benefits over the years.

Final Software Solution Selection: The final selection is based on cost benefit analysis and recommendations made by stakeholders. In addition to the cost benefit analysis, other factors such as features of the software package, its ability to be configured or customized to accommodate the organization's current and future needs, extendibility, etc., are significant in making the final decision. [Frankel, 1986] [Hollander, 2000]

154. How do you assess solution options? Understanding solution and organizational needs and constraints (limitations)

Continuing to the previous answer, this will include evaluating each software solution (software packages or customized software solution build either by the in-house team or an external vendor)

There are a few more criteria to be considered in making the final solution selection. The following is a partial list of these criteria.

a. **Features and functionalities:** Does the software package or software solution meet the organizational and the stakeholders' needs? Is the proposed solution capable of adapting the new changes or needs? How much can the proposed solution be extended in terms of capacity and quality requirements to accommodate future requirements?

b. **Data requirement:** What are the data requirements? Does the proposed solution meet that data and report requirement?

c. **Organizational capability to implement the solution:** What are the organization's current capabilities? What are the gaps adopting proposed solution? Do these gaps require additional budget to adopt the new solution?
d. **Cost of the solution and cost of the ownership:** What is the cost of the solution? What are the combined costs of building and implementing the solution? What is the total cost of ownership, i.e., the cost of building, implementing, and operating the solution? Sometimes the maintenance cost could be high and it may have a significant impact on the budget over the years.
e. **Time to implement:** What is the timeline to implement the software solution? The software packages may require less time compared to customized solution. However, additional customization required in ready-made packages may require substantial time that needs to be considered.
f. **Post implementation support:** What is the post-implementation support needed? This includes the number of employees, operational costs, and suppliers' annual maintenance cost, etc.

155. How do you define performance measures for a solution and recommend the action to increase the solution value?

The performance measurement can be defined as part of the non-functional requirement. Please refer to performance testing in the business analysis know-how testing section.

To increase the solution value, the IT team can provide additional requirements stated in nice-to-have or requirements that are specified under the "desire" category. In addition, the solution value can increase if it is adaptable and expandable to accommodate future needs.

4.4 Change Management:

156. What is change management for the business analyst?

Change management is a part and parcel of the software development process because it is not possible to anticipate all the requirements in the early stage due to the business dynamics or solution evolution process. The previous sections described the process of initiating change and seeking necessary approvals for them.

Approvals are analyzed and planned for implementation. They are assigned to the team member, who will in turn coordinate with all relevant teams to develop, test, and implement the change. Once the change is validated against the requirement, it is formally signed-off, communicated, and closed.

The change related information is integrated into configuration management, change request management, status, and measurement management. [Bolles, 2002].

The change management policy defined is largely based on the project, organization standards and stakeholders' comfort covering the following areas:
1. Configuration Management
2. Change Management
3. Designing Configuration and Information Management

157. How do you recognize the need for change? OR What is the basic information required in initiating the Change Request?

It may contain the following basic information:

ID	Date	Title	Description	Rational	Initiator	Priority
(Unique Identifier)	The date on which change was requested	Change Request Title	The description of the change in short and specific.	Why the change is necessary	A person who initiated the change	Priority of the change request
CRF020510	July 12, 2015	Incorporate additional security	Update the change to incorporate additional security	-8/10 banks have implemented it recently -it provides additional security feature -Increase in brand value -Increased customer trust.	Credit Card Manager	High

Additional Information:

#	Change Validator	Impact Analysis Status	* CCB Status	CCB Priority	Change Assigned To	Release Details
	Person checks if the change is new and valid	Justified /unjustified/need more details	Approved /not approved /under review	CCB's decision on priority	Person's name	When it will be implemented

(*CCB: Change Control Board)

158. How to initiate change request:

- With basic information mentioned above, the change request is initiated
- The reviewers will review the basic details to ensure the change request details are correct.
- The initial analysis is conducted to understand if change request is accepted or rejected.
- Once the change request is accepted, it is informed to the initiator (s) and the further process begins.
- Impact Analysis: The impact on cost and schedule is analyzed and presented to the business team to review the value of the change request.
- Based on the impact analysis, the business team will conduct the benefit vs. risk analysis before deciding on the change request.
- Assess and evaluate the Request for Change (RFC) against the benefit vs. risk analysis.

- Matrix for evaluating the change

#	Item	Benefit	Risk	Decision
1	RFC1/C1	5	0	Yes
2	RFC2 /C2	4	3	Yes
3	RFC3 /C3	0	5	Yes
4	RFC4 /C4	2	1	No
5	RFC5 / C5	0	0	No

*Request for Change (RFC)

a. Setting a vision for change: What and how and when it should be completed and its significance on the project/solution or overall business.
b. Understanding the dynamics: What is the change? How is it connected to the overall solutions? What are the dependencies and how are they connected? And finally, who will be involved in impact analysis.
c. Assigning the change: Assigning the change to a person or group based on the person's expertise.
d. Identifying a change approach
e. Planning the change
f. Review RFC (request for change)
   i. If not successful, review and check the issue and re-implement –> if not successful –> back out –> post implementation review –> close RFC
   ii. Authorized Request for Change (RFC) –> accept –> plan for initial impact analysis –> validate the RFC –> create RFC –>
   Technical review and sing-off.
   After signing off the RFC, following process can be followed to implement and close the change request.
   - Definition: Defining the change
   - Development: Developing the change
   - Implementation: Implementing the change

- Controlling the change process
- Evaluation: Evaluating the change
- Learning: Learning the change

iii. Not authorized Request for Change (RFC) –> review –> accept/reject –> if accepted, follow II process (mentioned above) –> create RFC or if rejected, provide explanation –> close RFC.

159. What are the different types of changes?

The following are the different types of changes:

Changes take place due to various reasons. Some changes occur due to incorrect or incomplete requirements. Sometimes, requirements are correct, but they evolve through the project and, hence, need to be updated.

Most of the large projects implemented through many releases over the year(s) face this situation where requirements derived in the first place are no longer suitable or needed or valid due to the dynamic nature of the business environment. Most of the changes occur due to the need to remain updated or having an edge over competitors.

Changes occurring due to these reasons must be considered and updated to make the solution relevant in every aspect.

Fixing "incorrect" requirements

- The corrections can be further categorized into urgent (hotfix) change or corrective requirements that need to be fixed or corrected.

- If the system failure occurs due to incorrect requirements, it may be referred to as an error. These "requirements" are to be corrected using fixing code or through an implementation of technical corrective measures. If it is a hotfix or urgent, it must be attended to without any further delay.

Fixing "incomplete" requirements

- Sometimes requirements remain incomplete due to a variety of factors such as overseeing the dependencies, new situations/requirements or any other changes. These requirements must be completed with additional change/requirements and implemented, depending on their priority and urgency.

- Fixing outdated requirements: Since most requirements are derived in the early stages of a project and take a long time to implement, a revision is required to validate their relevance. Business is dynamic due to fast-paced technology changes being incorporated to gain a competitive edge over other players. These changes can vary from low to high on urgency level. Any change associated with the brand image or directly related to financial gain or loss, automatically become high on priority and urgency, irrespective of the status of requirement.

160. Describe the change control board.

The change control board is formed with stakeholders, subject matter experts (SMEs, from both technical as well as domain), business analysts, project managers, and coordinators to manage, and control the changes effectively throughout the project.

#	Role	Responsibilities
1	Change Manager	Managing & controlling change management process
2	Stakeholders	Monitoring and controlling impact of change on solution
3	Product Manager	Monitoring and Controlling the impact of change on products
4	Domain SMEs	Provide input on their domain to assess the change
5	Sponsor	Assessing benefit vs. risk and approving budget for change

6	Project Manager	Monitoring overall change in terms of technical and other issues
7	Business Analyst	Key coordinator and facilitator to handle the change throughout its life cycle.
8	Contractor	Provide input on the impact on budget and schedule due to the change.
9	Architect	Providing the input on possible impact on solution architect or stability.
10	Technical Lead/Developer	Providing inputs on the work associated with change.
11	User representatives	User inputs on handling their comfort
12	Customer Representatives	To ensure that change is acceptable
13	QA Lead	Observing the impact on other requirements and providing the input on the work associated with the change
14	Configuration Manager	Ensuring all the change and impact related data are stored for the future use.
15	Implementation SME	Ensure that the change is in-line with current technical needs of user environments.
16	Database representative	Any change in existing database, structure or any additional database related requirements needed
17	Contractor representative	Ensuring smooth coordination and communication during and after change is implemented
18	Infrastructure SME	Ensure that infrastructure requirements, if any, are addressed.

161. What is impact analysis?

Impact analysis is part of the change management process. Whenever a new change or modification to the existing requirement is made, it requires analyzing the impact of change on the project and business. There are two types of impact analysis.

    a. Impact on budget and schedule, and
    b. Impact on business (benefits and risk analysis).

a. Budgets and Schedule:

The project management team will calculate the impact on budget and schedule. The project manager will provide the overall impact on the project and other dependencies arising due to the new change request, along with options to develop and deploy the solution. This information will help the business stakeholders to decide on whether to accept or reject the proposed change.

b. Benefits and Risks:
The business stakeholders evaluate the benefits in terms of tangible and intangible to justify the change.

Stakeholders also evaluate the risks that are associated with the change if the change is not approved or delayed. The risk can be categorized in terms of business and technology, and in both tangible and intangible ways.

The business risk could be a loss of image, trust, or loss of finance. It could also result in a penalty that has a significant impact on finances and brand image. For example, if the requirements have a bug in terms of some business loophole or process that could possibly result in financial loss due to the potential opportunity for malpractice, it could result in a regulatory penalty.

The technical issue could be associated with loss of data, privacy, or getting into trouble with the law enforcement. For example, handling credit card data or patients' data in new solutions.

The cost vs. benefits and benefits vs. risk along with the impact analysis must be carried out with diligence in the presence of respective subject matter experts (SMEs) to get a complete understanding of the possible future situations, risks, and other factors to make the decision.

PROJECT COST

PROJECT COST	FREQUENCY	DETAILS	Amount (in million$)
Hardware Capital Cost	Additional servers, networking	One-time	.30
Software development and	Project Manager, Business Analyst,	One-time	.80

project staff	Technical Team, Testing Team		
Licensed Software Cost	Software	One-Time	.50
Total Project Cost			1.6 M

RETURN ON INVESTMENT

Without Online Banking Solution (OBS)

The projected earnings for the bank without implementing the online banking solution are given below:

#	PARTICULARS	YEAR 1	YEAR 2	YEAR 3	YEAR 4	YEAR 5
a	No. of Customers	1.00	1.04	1.08	1.12	1.17
b	No. of Transactions	10.00	10.50	11.03	11.58	12.16
c	Gross Revenue	25.00	26.50	28.09	29.78	31.56
d	Expenses	10.00	11.00	12.10	13.31	14.64
e	Profit Before Tax (c-d)	15.00	15.50	15.99	16.47	16.92
f	Tax @35%	5.25	5.43	5.60	5.76	5.92
g	Profit After Tax (e-f)/ Free cash	9.75	10.08	10.39	10.70	11.00

Assumptions:
- Customer base is expected to grow @ 4%
- Transactions are expected to grow @ 5%
- Gross Revenue is expected to grow @ 6%
- Expenses are expected to grow @ 10%

With Online Banking Solution (OBS)

#	PARTICULARS	Y 1	Y 2	Y 3	Y 4	Y 5
a.	No. of Customers	1.00	1.10	1.21	1.33	1.46
b.	No. of Transactions	10.00	11.10	12.32	13.68	15.18
c.	Gross Revenue	25.00	27.00	29.16	31.49	34.33
d.	Expenses	10.00	10.60	11.24	11.91	12.62
e.	Gross Profit	15.00	16.40	17.92	19.58	21.70
f.	Capital Investment for Online Marketing	1.60				

g.	Depreciation on Online Banking	0.00	0.40	0.40	0.40	0.40
h.	Profit before tax (e-g)	15.00	16.00	17.52	19.18	21.30
i.	Tax @35%	5.25	5.60	6.13	6.71	7.46
j.	Profit after tax (h-j)	9.75	10.40	11.39	12.47	13.85
k.	Add: Depreciation	0.00	0.40	0.40	0.40	0.40
l.	Free Cash Flow	9.75	10.80	11.79	12.87	14.25

162. How to process recommendations and approvals?

The changes are part of the software development process. The previous question described the process of initiating change and seeking approvals for them.

The approval is analyzed and later scheduled for implementation. They are assigned to the team member who will, in turn, coordinate with all relevant teams to develop, test and implement the change. Once the change is validated against the requirement, it is formally signed-off, communicated, and closed.

The change related information is integrated into configuration management, change request management, status, and measurement management. [Bolles, 2002].

163. What roles do business analysts play during Change Management?

Depending on his role and responsibilities, a business analyst can play a vital role in change management in defining or customizing the existing change management policy, change control board (CCB), and the change management process for the project.

The business analyst provides inputs for impact analysis (impact of change on the schedule and budget) and risk vs. benefits analysis to make a decision.

164. How do you handle the change-request?

The following template is used in creating a change request while also providing an insight into the process of handling the change-request. It can be modified as necessary.

Item	Description
# or Unique Number	Unique Identifier for change-request (you can append it to requirement ID).
Title	Change-request title/short description in 2-3 words.
Description	Description of change-request in 2-3 lines.
Dependency	Is change interlinked with other requirements?
Rational	Justification for the change request.
Submission Date	Date change-request is submitted.
Requested By	Name of person who initiated change-request.
Priority	Priority of change-request. (0-5) or (High/Medium/Low).
Reviewed By	Name of person who reviewed 'change-request'.
Technical Impact Analysis	Impact on schedule and budget.
Business Impact Analysis	List benefits of accepting change-request. List of risk inherent in rejecting 'change-request'.
Change Control Board (CCB) Recommendation	Details of discussion of impact analysis and subsequent decision on how and when the change will be implemented.
Priority Update	New priority if needed/changed.
Accountable	Name of person(s) who will be accountable for developing and deploying change.
Post-Implementation Review	Description of review of post-implementation change-request.
Close-Out Approver	Name of person/s who approved/closed-out the 'change-request' review and approval process

Change-request process

Change Request: This process enables users to raise a change request and submit it. The change control board undertakes its initial review before accepting or rejecting it. Once accepted, a request for change (RFC) document is created.

The diagram shows the process of reporting the change-request, change management, change implementation and configuration.

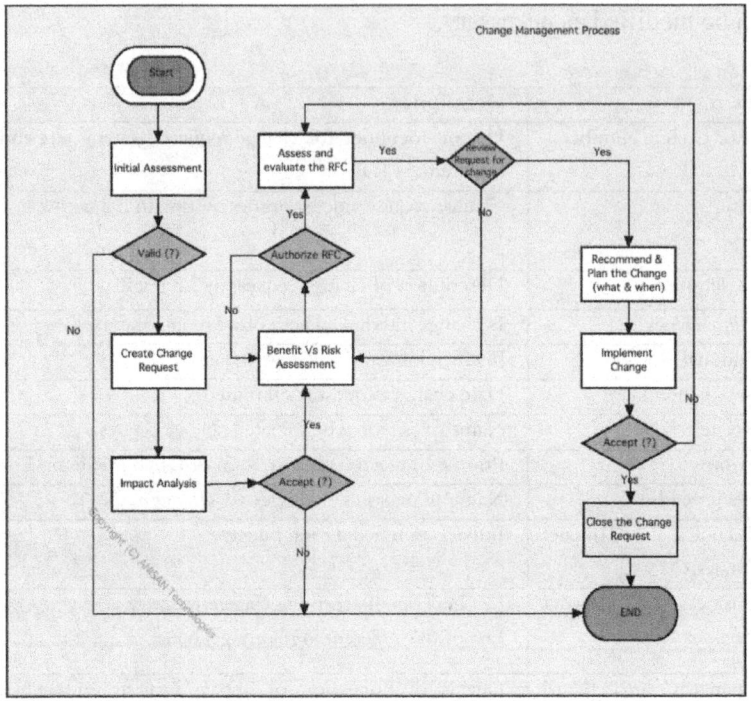

*RFC – Request for Change

Change Request: This process enables users to submit a change and the CCB team to undertake its initial review before accepting or rejecting it. Once accepted, a request for Change (RFC) document is created.

Change Management: Once an RFC is accepted, the request goes through impact analysis as mentioned in the template. Technical analysis is conducted in terms of impact on schedule and budget. The business impact analysis is conducted based on benefit vs. risk analysis to decide whether the change is justified against benefits it brings in or risks it poses to the business in future.

Change Analysis: Once a request for change (RFC) is accepted, the request goes through impact analysis as mentioned in the template.

Technical analysis is conducted in terms of its impact on schedule and budget. The business impact analysis is conducted based on benefit vs. risk analysis to decide whether the change is justified against benefits it brings in or risks it poses to the business in the future.

Technical Impact Analysis:
　a.　Impact on schedule and budget is estimated and presented for business stakeholders.

Business Impact Analysis:
　a.　Benefits: List benefits tangible and intangible benefits of accepting and implementing the change.
　b.　Risk: List of business and technical risks if the change is rejected.

Recommendations and Approvals: The recommendation is made based on the criticality of the change, project schedule, and risk perspective.

Change Implementation: This phase provides details of the change to be incorporated in the schedule, considering its nature in terms of priority or urgency and resource availability.

Once the change is implemented, it is reviewed and approved before being closed. If there is an issue with the change that requires it to be rolled back, it will be withdrawn before closing it out.

Close Change & Update Log: The change coordinator has to update the change details in the relevant project documents. [Bolles, 2002].

165.　How to prioritize or classify change?

Change can be classified based on its urgency or nature.

Corrective: Corrective changes involve fixing the error at the requirement stage.

Adoptive: The adoptive changes consist of adopting or applying new change(s) to a requirement that may have arisen due to changes in system boundary, business process, or technology.

Exceptional Change: Exceptional change involves anything that needs to be fixed urgently. It could be adoptive or corrective.

Or they can be classified as below:
- Normal Change
- Significant Change (High-Risk)
- Major Change
- Minor Change
- Standard Change (Pre-Approved)
- Expedited Change (Short-Interval)
- Emergency Change [Pohl, Rupp, 2011]

166. What is Configuration Management?

The configuration management system facilitates structuring, storing, and providing the project information to the project team in a systematic manner. The project information includes artifacts regarding requirements templates, documents, models, etc., that are under version control, clearly visible, and easily accessible to the authorized user. The changes to the information are tracked, stored, and secured methodically. It must provide detailed reports of the access and modification to any documents or artifacts stored within. The configuration management also supports defining the relationship among requirements that can be used to track the dependencies before, during, and after the change is processed.

The configuration may have one of more information associated with the requirement.

a. Storage: Where is the requirement stored?

b. Accessibility: What is the access role for individual requirement(s)?
c. Unique identification: How artifacts are identified?
d. Dependencies or logical connection: How requirements are connected?
e. Version: How the change in the document is stored with different versions?
f. Relationship: How are the requirements related to other requirements?

167. How do you verify the confirmed requirement(s)?

The confirmed requirements are referred to the requirements that are elicited, documented, and confirmed by the source of its origin.

You may use following checklist or customize as necessary to verify the confirmed requirements.

- They must have unique numbers, storage or retrieval process and rollback (if any) and other processes must be in-line with organizational standards
- They must be logically connected
- They must have correct details
- They must be consistent
- The individual requirement must be complete in itself
- They must be feasible, testable, and measurable against the specified parameters.
- If any changes are made to the requirements, they must be reflected upon and recorded appropriately with new version numbers.
- They must be verified against the checklist (if any). They must be verified against each parameter mentioned in the checklist to ensure the overall quality of the requirements.
- They must be validated against the solution scope and organizational objective(s).

4.5 Requirement Elicitation Techniques

168. What are major requirement elicitation techniques?
The followings are requirement elicitation techniques:

   a. Stakeholder Interview
   b. Document Analysis
   c. Questionnaire and Survey
   d. Facilitated Workshop
   e. Focused Group
   f. Prototypes
   g. Observations
   h. Creative Techniques: Brainstorming, mind mapping and scorecard

a. Stakeholder Interviews

Stakeholder interviews are one of the primary elicitation techniques. It is useful when a stakeholder has a significant amount of information to contribute or the requirement contains confidential details that cannot be shared in a group or the requirement doesn't have significant dependencies that require collaboration with other stakeholders.

Pros: It is useful to conduct an interview session having open-ended questions and later more information can be investigated by drilling answers to the next detailed level. The personal interaction involved helps in enhancing the quality of inputs.

The quantity of requirement: The investigator must be prepared with sufficient domain knowledge and questionnaires to make meaningful queries. It helps provide mile-wide and inch-deep information, i.e., significant details.

Cons: The downside of interview technique is, it is time consuming, expensive, and slow in comparison to other techniques. In a large size project, it is difficult to conduct several interviews. If the information or requirements were interlinked, it might be difficult to align differing or contradictory views that might impact on the quality of requirement.

b. Requirement Workshop
When the proposed solution is complex and involves many stakeholders and system owners, the requirement workshop is one of the most effective ways of eliciting requirements. The requirement workshop is a faster, comprehensive, and qualitative method.

The workshop helps the stakeholders to conduct a systematic session in formal or semi-formal or informal setting, where every stakeholder is scheduled, provided the agenda, and assigned parts based on his roles and responsibilities.

The facilitator keeps the team in collaborative and communicative mode. It also ensures that the team remains focused and contributes effectively towards requirement and related details.

The well-organized sessions will include various other elicitation and analysis techniques such as "mind mapping", "process diagram", and "functional decomposition" to elicit, elaborate, and finalize the requirements. For that, the facilitator plans for a smart board, software tools, and other supporting materials for elicitation. A scribe is appointed to document every data related to the discussion for future reference.

To complete requirement elicitation activity, more than one workshop may be needed to collaborate with all stakeholders. In addition to this, more sessions may be required to elaborate, present, prioritize, and model the elicited requirements before signing them off in a formalized structure.

Pros: This formal and well-structured elicitation technique keeps everyone focused and encourages effective collaboration. This session can help in reducing the elicitation time needed requirement and elicitation result confirmation as most of the work related to elicitation, analysis, review, and confirmation could be completed in these workshops. Since most stakeholders (business as well as technical) are part of the session, the requirements can be analyzed from different perspectives, discussed, and finalized.

This formal workshop helps to define current state and future state in a group meeting by bringing most of the stakeholders on to the same platform to collaborate and confirm. It also removes misunderstandings and ambiguity (if any) regarding requirement and helps in building consensus.

Modelling techniques such as Activity Diagram, Class Diagram, Use Cases, and State Diagram may be useful to bring everyone on the same level of understanding.

Cons: It requires an experienced and skilled professional to conduct the workshop. In the absence of a skilled and tactful business analyst, there is a possibility of a chaotic situation ensuing. In addition, bringing many stakeholders together may be a challenging task, especially if stakeholders are dispersed or the senior ranking stakeholders are overshadowed. Some stakeholders may not be comfortable in contributing in a group setting due to their personal temperament or nature of their roles. Therefore, if the requirement is elicited forcefully, that may result in an incomplete or incorrect assessment of requirement, affecting their overall quality.

If the business analyst or stakeholders are not comfortable with modelling techniques, an additional explanation or alternate technique may be required.

c. Contract-Style Requirement List
The contract-style requirement list is one of most effective ways of documenting requirements.

Creating a list of requirements is one of the usual ways in this technique to avoid the document from running into a few hundred pages. Specifying requirements in bullet points or in a list helps the audience to stay focused. Additional description documents can be used to support these requirements.

Pros: The concise and focused list of requirements helps avoid unnecessary descriptions if stakeholders are already well versed with the domain. It provides an overview of the system for comprehension.

Cons: It is difficult to track the items in a list or derive a picture if the list becomes too long. The requirement may provide different perspectives on a high-level and on a detail-level. It may provide partial or different views of the solution through the list to different stakeholders, and that could potentially result in confusion and conflict in the absence of detailed supportive document(s). This may impede the system architect from producing the system designs and other related descriptions.

If the requirements in the list are not adequately prioritized or traced with other requirements, it may lead to an obscured view of requirement architecture and context to the solution. It provides a misleading impression of the solution and its nature unless the requirements are comprehensively connected. Failure to trace the requirement may result in the requirement undergoing several changes, leading to more conflict due to re-negotiations.

d. Prototypes

This used to be a very popular Requirement Elicitation technique in the 1980s. To this day, it continues to be a preferred technique among technical stakeholders. Prototypes in IT are models or replicas of existing or future systems, used to communicate requirements among stakeholders. It significantly enhances the stakeholders' understanding of the solution and ability to visualize a future system. This is a powerful technique to understand features of the existing system and suggest enhancements based on that. It reduces the gap between two stakeholders while communicating the requirement and its implementation. When a stakeholder can visualize the future system by seeing its prototype, he can both make suggestions and negotiate without having to wait for the system to be implemented. This way, changes are incorporated in the early stages of the project cycle, i.e., in the requirement or design phase, helping to significantly reduce costs and lead to faster delivery of the system.

Pros: The complete prototype improves the understandings of the stakeholder regarding the future solution. This also reduces eventuality of any confusion arising later in the initial stage itself. Any improvements, if needed, can be incorporated at an early stage to improve quality of the end product.

Cons: Too much focus on the prototype may lead to the loss of actual requirement or requirement details pertaining to middleware and the backend. That could lead to more complications. A smart business analyst needs to balance it well. Designers or technical teams may feel pressurized to use the prototype to integrate with their technical work. Someone passionate about the prototype may waste too much time on that at the peril of ignoring the core requirements. Furthermore, stakeholders, mistaking the prototype for the actual solution may be under the misimpression that the solution is ready. In such a scenario, they may get impatient about the final delivery.

e. Use Cases

The use case is used to describe the particular functionality of an existing or potential solution. It captures an interaction between an external user and the system to generally achieve a particular business goal or functionality. The system response is dependent on the role the user plays in the organization. For example, if the user is a customer, he will be able to interact with the system as a customer to achieve the goals. However, he cannot access other user accounts. If the user is a system administrator, the user will interact with the system as a system administrator and may have access to an entire system, including the access to other users. This access is dependent on his role as a system administrator. However, if the same user (the system administrator) logs-in as a customer, as mentioned earlier, the access to other users is disabled.

A high-level use case is used to define the software system scope. (Please refer to the use case section for more details.)

Use case is a deceptively simple tool for describing the behavior of a software solution. A use case contains a textual description. It is a way for the intended users to work with the software through its interface. Use case does not describe the internal workings of a software solution nor does it explain the process of implementation. It simply shows the steps that the user follows to interact the software solution to complete his work. All of the ways that the users interact with the software can be described in this manner.

Since the 1990s, use case has rapidly evolved to become the most common practice for capturing functional requirements since it is not object orientated in nature.

Each use case focuses on describing how to achieve a single business goal or task. A use case describes just one feature of the system. For most software projects this means that multiple, perhaps dozens, of use cases, are needed to fully detail the new system. The degree of formality of a particular software project and its stage will influence the level of detail required in each use case.

A use case explains the interactions between external actors and the system under consideration to accomplish a particular business goal. Actors are the users who interact with the system from outside the system boundary. An actor can be a class of users, roles users play or other systems.

A use case explains the interaction between system and external actors to achieve a specified business goal. The actors can be user or class of users, system, or timer who is interacting with the system from outside the system boundary.

(Please refer to the use case section for more details.)

A use case should:

- Describe a business task to serve a business goal
- Have no implementation-specific language
- Be at the appropriate level of detail
- Be short enough to be implemented by a single software developer in a single release.
- A use case can be very good for establishing the functional requirements; however, it is not suited to capturing non-functional requirements. [Stellman and Greene, 2005] [Hossain and Hasan, 2006] [Jacobson, Christerson et al. 1992] [Cockburn 2002]

f. Questionnaire and Survey
Questionnaire

Sir Francis Galton, an English polymath, was the first one to introduce this methodology. Today, questionnaires are an important instrument of surveys. A questionnaire has a typical set of questions eliciting ideas, behaviors, preference, attitudes, data, and many more details.

Questionnaires can be completed in a variety of ways: in-person, telephonic interviews, door-to-door, or online.

In today's digitally dominated world, online surveys have become the most popular mode of data collection. The survey could be done in a formal or an informal setting, with topics ranging from trying to understand the current mood of nation on a certain issue, or employee feedback or preferences, or the customer feedback on certain products or services.

A survey must follow statistical principles for creating sample data, defining target groups, and representing the survey results.

The Survey Process
It is a methodical way of collecting data from targeted populations that can be used for statistical or quantitative research purposes. Since it is highly methodical, proper planning is vital to succeed in the process.

Before undertaking a survey, survey conductors must systematically plan the process. The followings are some of the items that need to be considered before conducting a survey.

Purpose of the Survey: This should answer why a survey needs to be conducted. What data needs to be collected and why? Who is the target audience? What is the survey method? What are the questions and their expected answers (if they are objective in nature)? Who will administer the survey? Do they need the training to conduct and administer the survey? How will the data be collected? How and where will the data be stored? Who will access the data? Who will assess and analyze the data? How will the results be produced? How the results will be presented? Whom will the results be presented to? What, where, and how the results will be used? How the data and results will be archived for future use? [Elporable.com and Wiley online library] [Marr, 2015]

g. Observation:
This is one of the powerful techniques to capture data or requirements in an active or inactive manner. One of the methods of doing research is to ask people questions. This is most people's concept of what a survey will involve. However, it is possible to conduct research without asking questions by simply observing the respondents. This is called observation.

There are two ways of conducting observations: Formal and Informal observation.

a. Informal observation: It is also known as an unstructured or an exploratory observation. It is done when the research group has insufficient data or knowledge of a population. The main reason for informal observation is to create hypotheses to be tested later in a survey or using formal observations. The observer may collect the data they observe and analysis may be conducted depending on the data collected at that stage.

The observer may collect the data they observe and analysis may be conducted depending on the data collected at that stage.

b. Formal observation: Formal observations are structured or systematic. They are similar to a survey, where every respondent is asked the same set of questions, but with the difference that direct questions are not asked. Instead, particular types of behavior are sought out and counted. The observer needs to plan and create a set of questionnaires to capture the data.

A business analyst can seek an appointment with the stakeholder or the end users operating the existing system to understand the current state (As-Is). This is an accurate method to capture the requirements effectively, especially when users have no time to provide the data or they are not motivated enough to fill out information or participate in the requirement workshop. This is also effective for gathering the information related to processes, business rules, and handling exceptions when a user is interacting with the software solution.

Active Mode: The business analyst can ask questions on various processes or policies the users deal with in their day-to-day work.

Passive Mode: The business analyst does not ask questions on processes or policies while observing users and their work. The focus is entirely on data collection.

Automatic Observation: In this method, users' interaction with the software solution can be captured by the software application to understand their interaction, behavior, and techniques in handling the solution.

It can be done either manually on paper or through an audio-visual recording mode.

Combining observation and response
When you are studying people's behavior, observation can produce more accurate results than asking respondents what do they do. However, observing behavior alone does not always tell you the reasons for people's actions. So, to understand your audience well, the best data comes from combining observation and other research methodologies.

   i. Creative Techniques: Brainstorming, Mind Mapping and Scorecard

[Rowel and Alfeche, 1997] [Kotonya, Sommenville, 1998]

5 Requirement Verification and Validation

"Computer scientists call validation: whereas verification asks "Did I build the system right?," validation asks "Did I build the right system?"
— *Max Tegmark, Life 3.0: Being Human in the Age of Artificial Intelligence*

5.1 Requirement Qualities

169. What are the main parameters or qualities?
OR
How to verify and validate requirements?

The requirements must be verified and validated to consider them as good requirements.

The following are the techniques to verify the quality of requirements.
- 5C
- SMART
- Checklist
- Customized Verification Process

5C
Check if a requirement is complete, clear, consistent, configurable (modifiable) and confirmed (and approved by stakeholders).

SMART
Check if a requirement is SMART:
    S – Specific: Is it "specific"?
    M – Measureable: Is it "measurable"?
    A – Attainable: Is it attainable?
    R – Relevant: Is it "relevant"?
    T – Timely: Can it be achieved in a specific "time"?

Checklist:
In addition, we can check if every requirement is verified against predefined parameters such as:

- Agreed: Agreed upon by stakeholders

- Ranked: Ranked based on various parameters such as business value (tangible and intangible), reliability, and ease of implementation.
- Unambiguous: It is not subject to multiple interpretations.
- Doable: It can be developed, tested, and implemented.
- Traceable: It can be traced to original as well as derived requirements.
- Checklist: The requirements must pass the basic criteria mentioned in the checklist.

Customized Verification Process:
A company may have a specific checklist or standard process to verify quality of requirements. If not, the business analyst can create one using parameters that are suitable for the proposed solution.

Validation: Every requirement and its value are validated against the business need and business case. This is done to ensure that every requirement is part of the project need to ensure that it contributes to the overall project, and contributes to the organizational goals.

170. What are the parameters of good requirement documentations?
As per IEEE std. 830-1998, the followings are the criteria for good requirement documentation.

- Unambiguous: The requirement document must be unambiguous, i.e., it should not be subject to multiple interpretations.
- Well-Defined Structure: It should have a well-defined structure that represents the information in clear, logical, and consistent form.
- Modifiability and Extendibility: The document needs to be modifiable and extendible depending on the need and relevance.

- Completeness: The completeness of the requirement document ensures that all relevant information is included in the document.
- Consistency: The requirement document is logically connected, and the data list indexed appropriately.
- Traceability: The document has the proper version and history section where all the document versions and their details are listed to understand how the document has evolved over a period of time.

171. What is software solution (application) usability?

It is to know if the software solution is intuitive, easy to navigate, helpful in finding information and appealing. The end users can use the software solution without any external help such as customer service or a help menu. For instance, when we start using a new smartphone, we quickly or intuitively figure out how to use the phone, its features, and functionalities without having to take recourse to the help menu or calling up customer service.

172. What is user-centric design?

In this scenario, we understand the requirements from the user's point of view and design software solution (application) accordingly. Basic information about users, and their roles and responsibilities are defined in the stakeholder analysis. The features and functionalities are derived from their job role, responsibilities, and daily processes and activities. Another way is through documentation of user stories.

173. How do you transform business requirements to functional requirements?

Business requirement document defines the solution to business stakeholders. Why the solution is built (to address the problem or opportunity), features and functionality needed by business stakeholders to interact with the proposed solution and, lastly, how the proposed solution will resolve the identified business need.

For instance, the customer will transfer funds online from one of the accounts to another account within or outside the bank.

Meanwhile, functional requirements will elaborate what system should do to enable stakeholders to achieve their goal or interact with the solution. The functional requirement details may be provided in a structured description supported by graphics or models to reduce ambiguity and increase the understanding level of readers. The details may include unique ID, name, description, pre-condition, process, post-condition, success criteria, business rule, input/output data, model or model reference (if the models are stored in a separate file), and the comments section for additional details.

In addition, the functional requirement will have non-functional requirements to support the functionality.

For instance, the online banking solution provides customer with the option to select a beneficiary (if the beneficiary does not exist, a customer can add and validate the same) and select the account from where the funds will be transferred. It also allows the customer to enter the amount, verify transfer details against the business rules, and allows customer to confirm transfer, provide transfer details, and take a printout of the transaction.

174. Why do you need to re-visit the strategy analysis? Why you have to redefine business need or solution scope once the solution is defined?

The high-level business need and solution scope are defined at the initial stage. After completing analysis through the process of defining solution, the business need may change due to additional requirements, newly discovered dependencies, change in environment, and identification of capability gap. If the business needs change, the solution scope will also change. If solution scope changes, the business case (cost vs. benefit analysis and risk analysis) changes.

Therefore, it is essential for the business analyst to keep updating all relevant documents throughout the project lifecycle.

175. Why the right solution leads to business success?

Time and again it has been emphasized that solution assessment adds value to your business and is the key to your success. It means we need to check if the solution is right for the business. Earlier, business solution and models based on the standard and proven parameters were not found successful on many occasions. The reason has been attributed to clinging of these companies to age-old conventions.

An organization has to, therefore, adopt a thoroughly professional approach in finding solutions to the problem areas. At the same time, the solutions have to be right on their own and also on the whole. In short, the success of any project is directly proportional to the value-additions and values realized to the organization.

Finding the right solutions and bringing value-addition to the organization is the main task of the business analyst. The solutions cannot be generalized. He has to possess radical skills for solution implementation. A solution has to be exactly tailored to the problem at hand and is widely known as customization. The business analyst has to study the type of industry and the prevailing norms, apart from aspects such as products and services. A synopsis of the operational structure of the organization and its customers are further tools for identification of the right solution.

There are many routes to success and value additions. They are like desires. We have a world of things we desire, but the success comes only with the need for an analytical approach. The thought process starts with a showcase full of desires. For example, a travel portal wants to have seat selection as a requirement at the initial stage whereas the business analyst will have to make the client/stakeholder understand that it is a 'desire' category or future requirement, i.e., once the travel portal is built and implemented successfully in the production environment, they can take the 'desire' category requirement to enhance their solution in future. This way, the solution implementation with critical requirements can be managed within the scheduled cost and time.

The thought process then moves to maturity and leads to a need. The need to prune confusing expenses results in a study leading to analysis and, finally, the right solution. The process is both intelligent and effective in modern times.

Once the right solution is in place and the process gets implemented, the burden of escalating costs recedes just because the eyes are set on the end-effect and an assurance of positive value addition to the organization. This quantum is much more than the additional burden sustained.

The business analyst needs to highlight the value-additions brought in by his skills. It is the business analyst who has the upbeat skills to understand the inputs and deliverables applicable to individual client or customer. This alone can bring the desired success and true business value to any organization through the right solutions prescribed. [Jane, 2015]

176. How do you complete the post-implementation assessment?

The following sample post-implementation forms captures the key parameters regarding stakeholder feedback. This can be considered as a part of the formal feedback process and preserved for future reference such as audit, quality of the project management, lessons learned, etc.,

Verify software result.

Item	Question	Response
1.0	Do you agree that the developed solution is ready to be use?	Yes ☐ No ☐
1.2	Do you agree the implemented solution has adequately met the stated business goals and objectives?	Yes ☐ No ☐
1.3	Do you fully know and agree to accept all operational requirements including risks, maintenance costs, and other limitations as a result of ongoing operations?	Yes ☐ No ☐
1.4	Do you agree the project should be closed? If no, please explain:	Yes ☐ No ☐

Validate software solution outcome.

Item	Question	Response
	Rate the project outcome	
2.5	Solution Quality	Yes ☐ No ☐
2.6	Solution Performance	Yes ☐ No ☐
2.7	Solution Scope	Yes ☐ No ☐
2.8	Solution Cost (Budget)	Yes ☐ No ☐
2.9	Solution Schedule	Yes ☐ No ☐

6 Unified Modelling Language

"The secret to modeling is not being perfect. What one needs is a face that people can identify in a second. You have to be given what's needed by nature, and what's needed is to bring something new."

— *Karl Lagerfeld*

"You never change things by fighting the existing reality.
To change something, build a new model that makes the existing model obsolete."

— *R. Buckminster Fulle*

6.1 UML

The modelling language is defined by syntax and semantics. Syntax defines modelling elements, while semantics define the meaning of individual modelling elements and serve as the basis for their interpretation.

Conceptual modelling can be formal, informal, or semi-formal. However, logical modelling (for example data modelling) are based on structure, set of rules, and formal notations.

177. What is UML?
The Unified Modeling Language (UML) is the industry standard modelling language used for specifying, visualizing, modelling, documenting, developing, and communicating requirements. Besides, UML diagrams can also be used for depicting processes, architecture designs, and much more.

UML captures the structure and behavior of the requirement/function of the existing or to-be component. It uses industry standards notations, structure, set of rules, and diagrams to model the component to bring the team on the same level of understanding.

One of the primary objectives of UML is to reduce the ambiguity of documentation or textual description of the requirement or designs that may be subject to multiple interpretations.

Rational Software originally created the UML and the same is, now, maintained by OMG (Object Management Group). [UML 2.5, 2009]

178. What is the difference between system modelling and requirement modeling?

System modelling uses conventional modelling, while requirement modeling uses logical modelling.

System modeling illustrates systems and sub-systems, their components, their input-output and other details, while requirement modelling illustrates the specific requirement related to problem or features or function of the system.

179. What are the different UML models that are useful for the business analyst?

The following four types of UML diagrams are widely used by business analysts in the industry:

- Use Case Diagrams
- Activity Diagram
- Class Diagram
- State Diagram

Other diagrams are not used in this book as business analysts do not use them, so they are considered out of the scope.

The components of UML:

UML uses many components from different sources to model the requirement.

Structure: Actor, attributes, object, interface, class, package, and component.

Behavior: Activity, event, method, message, operation, use case(s), and state.

Relationship: Association, composition, aggregation (joint), disjoint, dependency, inheritance and other concepts.

180. How do we select the UML diagram to model requirement? Or which diagram is suitable to a particular requirement?

Use Case Diagram: High-level "use case" diagrams are created to illustrate the system overview to define system scope. And detailed "use case" illustrates a particular function/feature and how it interacts (reacts) to an external entity (actor – a user or system) in a particular event.

Activity Diagram: Activity diagram is used for illustrating the business process and sequence modelling of requirements or functions or use cases.

Class Diagram: Class diagram is used for data modelling and to illustrate the structure of the data with reference to system and system context. This is used to define the system context.

State Diagram: State diagram is used for illustrating the events, the behavior, and individual state as well as triggers that cause the transitioning between the states.

6.2 Use Case

181. What is the Use case?

A use case explains the interaction between the system and external actors to achieve a specified business goal. The actors could be a user, class of users, system, or timers that are interacting with the system from outside the system boundary.

This is one of the powerful techniques to capture data or information or requirements in an active or inactive manner. One way of conducting research is to ask people questions.

A use case is a software engineering technique for capturing potential requirements of an existing system, new system, or software change.

A high-level use case is used for defining the system scope and detailed level use is used for defining requirement.

A detailed use case is used for defining the specific functionality. It captures an interaction between the users and system, as well as the subsequent response to such interactions.

Each use case defines one or more "scenarios". It conveys how the system will interact with the end user or another system to achieve a specific business goal. Use cases usually avoid technical jargon, preferring the language of the end user or the business domain. Use cases can be co-authored by business analysts and end users.

In 1986, Ivar Jacobson, a noted contributor to the Unified Modeling Language (UML) and Unified Process, originated the concept of the use case. Jacobson's idea was influential and pivotal. Since then, many contributors added to the knowledge, but Alistair Cockburn made the most meaningful, prominent, and comprehensive contribution. He defined "what use cases are" and "how to write them effectively" in Writing Effective Use Cases, his widely popular book published in 2000.

Throughout the 1990s, use cases were one of the most common practices for capturing the functional requirements. This is because the use cases are not object-oriented in nature.

182. Explain scope and goals of a use case

A use case explains the interaction between the system and external actors to achieve a specified business goal. The actors could be a user, class of users, and system or timers that are interacting with the system from outside the system boundary.

This is one of the powerful techniques to capture the data or information or requirements in an active or inactive manner. One way of conducting research is to ask people questions.

Use cases consider the system as a "black box". The interactions with the system, i.e., user actions and the system responses to that action, are perceived from outside the system. This is a pre-defined policy to simplify the description of requirements and avoids getting into the trap of making assumptions on how this functionality will be implemented.

A use case should:
- Define a business task to serve a business goal
- Not have any implementation-specific language
- Be at the appropriate level of detail
- Be short enough to be implemented by one software developer in a single release.

183. What is the use case diagram?

As per OMG (2009), use case diagrams specify usage of the system by capturing the requirement in the form of what a system is supposed to do in a particular event.

When the external entities (Actors – people or system) interact with the system, the use case captures the interaction and the behavior of the system. Depending on the requirement, there could be one or more use cases created to define the behavior of the system.

184. What are the elements used in use cases?

Use Case: The "oval shape" is used to illustrate the use case.

The oval shape as an use case is shown in next page.

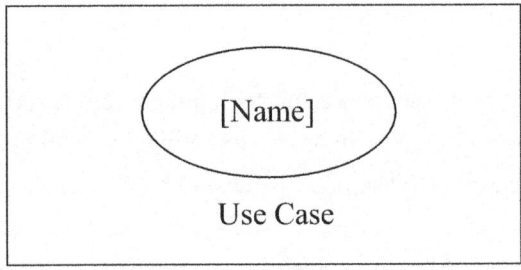

Fund Transfer: A customer should be able to transfer the fund online.

Name: Name of the use case is a verb or noun that describes the use case in two to four words.

To identify the use cases in the system, the following questions can be asked. [Schneider and Winters, 1998]:

- What functions will the actor want from the system?
- Does the system store information? What actors will create, read, update or delete this information?
- Does the system need to notify an actor about chances in the internal state?
- Are there any external events the system must know about? What actor informs to the system of those events?

185. Who is an "actor"?

Actors: External entity, i.e., outside the system boundary who interact with the system. It could be a person or system. There are four types of actors: human, system, hardware, and timer.

A person or a system can be an "actor" as shown in next page.

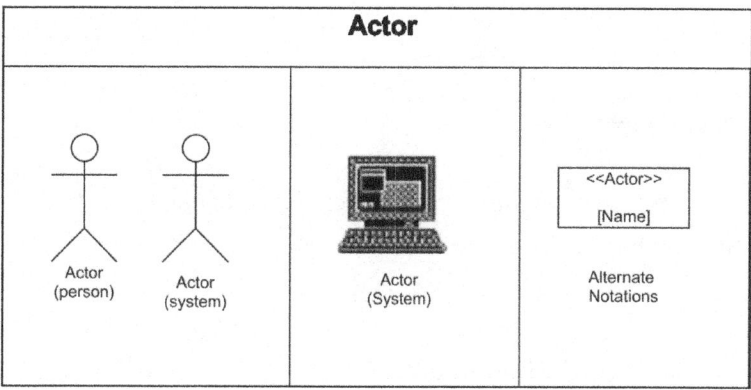

Actor: customer and system

To identify actors of the system, the following questions can support the process. [Schneider and Winters, 1998]:
- Who uses the system?
- Who installs the system?
- Who starts up the system?
- Who maintains the system?
- Who shuts down the system?
- What other systems use this system?
- Who gets information from this system?
- Who provides information to the system?
- Does anything happen automatically at a present time?

186. What is system boundary?

Name of use case can be used to define the boundary of the system that separates the actor and system. The following notation can be used to create a system boundary.

```
┌─────────────────────────┐
│  [Name]                 │
│                         │
│                         │
│                         │
└─────────────────────────┘
```

System Boundary

For example, "online fund transfer" is the boundary that will replace [Name] in the diagram.

187. What is the flow of event?

As mentioned in the previous answer, the use case assists stakeholders in visualizing a system. Besides the use case diagram, the textual description of the sequential flow of events of a use case is equally important to understand the use case clearly. This description supports the flow description of what actually happens in a use case. This is well described in the use case template in question 188.

188. What is "extend" and 'included' relationship?

"Extend" Relation: It illustrates an optional extended function or the use case. It captures both a normal behavior, and an exception. The exception is captured in a separate use case.

For an example, the "Add Beneficiary" (or payee or recipient) option is the "extend" part of the use case or extended relationship. A customer can add the recipient before transferring the fund if the recipient (beneficiary) is not in the recipient list.

"Included" Relation: It illustrates a mandatory function or use case to complete the primary use case.

It is used in:
a. Valuation
b. Validate user interaction
c. Sanity check on sensor inputs
d. Check for proper authorization

For example, the business rule mentions the need of "security code" verification before completing a transfer. A software system generates and sends it as a text message to the customer's registered mobile phone. In turn, the customer enters the security code received on his mobile phone and the software system verifies the security code entered by the customer to ensure the security of the transaction, before completing the fund transfer.

In order to create a use case diagram, an author will have to refer to activity diagram, sequence diagram, communication diagram, and state machine diagram.

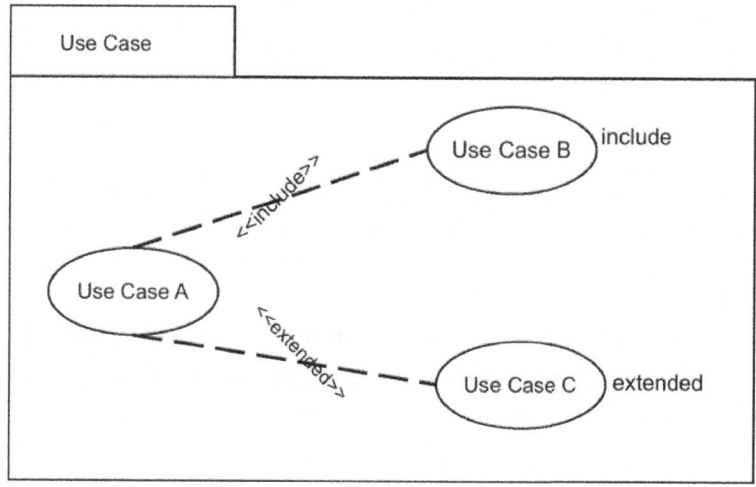

189. How to prepare the use case? Or How to write an effective use case?

Here is the brief process of creating use cases.

i. Degree of detailing

There are three levels of details mentioned in the book that can be used in creating use cases.

ii. Brief

As the name suggests, a brief summarizes the use case that is most suitable for use in a spreadsheet for planning or showing the overview of the use cases. The spreadsheet provides information in a tabular format.

#	Use Case	Description	Priority	Use case Diagram	Version No.	Comments
Unique ID	Name	Brief Description	Business priority (low/med/high/critical) or Ranking them 0-10	Brief diagram		
234	Online Fund Transfer	Allow the customer to transfer fund online	10	*[Fund Transfer use case diagram showing Customer, Fund Transfer, Verify Security Code, Add Beneficiary, System]*	2.0	NA

Casual

It comprises of a textual description of the use case that covers the items mentioned in the brief use case. It also elaborates the summary of the use case in the form of a story.

Detailed

A formal use case consists of an in-depth or complex use case description structured in a formal template. For creating a consistent view, the use cases in the project follow the similar structure that is easy to comprehend. This template is widely recognized as a use case or use case template.

Use cases are discussed in detail in the next section on use case templates.

Appropriate Detailing
Some software development methodologies do not require anything more than a simple use case to define requirements. However, some other development methodologies require detailed use cases to define requirements. For a large or complex project, it will be crucial to use detailed use cases.

The degree of details may vary, depending on the project and its progress or current state. At the initial stage, the use case may be concise, but they evolve as requirements progress from analysis, review, and confirmation stages.

The use cases progress from high-level to detailed level along with the advancement of the project. Initially, the key stakeholders and sponsors are keen in knowing a high-level scope through these use cases, and later user will review the semi-formal or more detailed level. However, the technical team needs complete specifications of these use cases when it starts working on a particular requirement.

Use Case Templates
There is no official or standard template for documenting the use cases. Some parameters that are considered as standard are widely used in the industry.

Most of the organizations that follow project management standards have a pre-defined standard use case template for the business analysts to use it. The business analyst can review this standard template and modify as per his needs.

Standard use case elements include:
- Use Case ID
- Use Case name
- Iteration
- Summary
- Preconditions
- Triggers
- Basic course of events
- Model (Use Case diagram)
- Alternative paths
- Post conditions
- Business rules
- Notes
- Author and date
- Also, some templates have additional elements that are useful to the technical team in implementing the requirements. These elements include assumptions, exceptions, recommendations, technical requirements, etc. There may also be industry-specific details or sections in the template.

Use Case ID: It is a unique identifier of a specific use case. For example, use case ID: 234.

Use Case Name
The name indicates the requirement or functionality or the feature. It is a noun or verb, goal-driven, and consists of two to four words. For example, "Fund Transfer," (or 'Transfer Fund') or "Account view" or "Login" etc. can be the use case names.

Iteration/Revision History
It states the background of the use case and also indicates how the use case has evolved over the time. It is important to maintain all the

versions of the use cases to refer for requirement evolution, change managements, and for all other purposes. At times, users may desire to review the perspective and refer to the older version of use cases to understand how and why the changes were made in functionality.

Summary

This is a use case summary consisting of two to four lines that provides a quick overview of the use cases to the reader. It helps users to decide whether to proceed further to read the entire use case or not. The summary provides 'what the use is all about', 'who are actors', and 'what is the main goal', etc.

Scope or System Boundary: The use case name can extend to the system boundary. The scope explains the components inside the use case and actors interacting with them from outside the system.

Anything out of the scope is also mentioned here.

Actors:

As mentioned in the previous section, the actors are the users who interact with the system from outside the system boundary. Actors can be - human, system, hardware, and timer.

Model:

Models explain the use case having "include" and "extended" section if required.

Pre-conditions

If there is any condition(s) when the user interacts with the system or initiate the function (use case), this must be true to successfully execute the use case.

For example, the user must be logged-in into the banking system and must have sufficient balance to make the online transfer. But having mentioned this, the transfer will not initiate automatically if the user doesn't enter all the required inputs such as beneficiary details and transfer amount before clicking on the "confirm" button. Here, the "confirm" button is the trigger and not the pre-condition.

Triggers

The trigger is a condition, function, or event that initiates the action. It can be internal, external or temporal.

Basic course of events

Each use case should convey at least one primary scenario or usual course of events. The main basic course of events is frequently specified as an orderly set of steps. For example:
- The system prompts the user to log in
- The user enters his name and password
- The user submits the login credentials
- The system verifies the login information
- The system logs the user on to the system
- ...and so on.

Alternative paths:
A use case can have alternate or secondary paths that are different from the main path. It simply means there are alternate ways of achieving the goal.

An example of an alternative path would be:
- The system recognizes cookies on the user's machine.
- Go to step 4 (main path)

Another alternative path
- The user fails to enter correct user-ID or password
- System doesn't allow the user to login
- The user uses the forgot the password option
- The system sends the link to reset password

- The user uses the link in the mail to reset the password
- The user enters the system

Post-conditions

- Post-conditions explain the state after the use case scenario is complete.

Business Rules

Business rules are meant for a making decision in a particular situation or event. These business rules further guide the user or the system on how to select an option and proceed to achieve the goal. It is based on an assumption and may apply to either single or multiple use case(s).

- After the third attempt, an Internet-based system locks the user out for 24 hours. This could be a generic rule applicable to all the users and user types, depending on the business or operational policies.
- A user email ID or other credentials must be updated and/or validated every year.

Notes

Notes are the additional details that are not part of the template. These could be unique and vital information regarding the use case that is useful to the user.

Stakeholders:

These are the stakeholders who will have a stake in the use case. Their inputs and/ or approvals are necessary to define use case. This may contain the list of stakeholders who will have either active or passive interest in the use case, depending on their role and responsibility in the organization.

Author and date

The author is the person who creates and documents the use cases. Sometime, the stakeholder who contributes significantly can also be the author. In such cases, it is a collaborative effort and the document is jointly owned. The author and author description constitute important information as the readers can reach out to the author in case of a doubtful situation.

The date is a very important part of the information that tells the reader about the history of the use case document. If the date is older than two to three years, the readers may want to check for the updated information, if any updates.

Use cases and the development process

Use cases are progressed as the development of the project proceeds. The use case format and development depend on the project management approach. For example, in agile, the use case may be brief and in a traditional or formal approach, it may be detailed, i.e., structured and documented them in a formal template. It is also dependent on the stakeholders' preferences.

In some approaches, use cases can initiate as brief business use cases, and later evolve or advance into more detailed system use cases, and then eventually progress into highly detailed and intensive test cases. [Cockburn, 2000]

190. What are the benefits of use case?
Use cases have several benefits.

- They are simple to create and easy to understand due to uniform format.
- They are agile and better for capturing requirements by avoiding large documentation.
- They complement the requirement description.
- They are easy to trace.

- They discourage premature design.
- They are reusable. They can be used through various stages of life cycle such as design, development, testing, and implementation phase, as well as for various other purposes.
- Use cases in agile format are suitable for capturing software requirements. They are often different from a large or massive document that struggles to communicate the actual requirements before construction of a new system begins. [Cockburn, 2000]

191. Describe the Use Case Template.

Overview of use cases:

You can use a tabular or Excel sheet to present an overview of use cases or catalogue to refer:

Use Case Identification and History [Name]			
Use Case ID:	01		
Use Case Name:	UC-01 Fund Transfer	Version No:	1.0
Use Case Diagram:	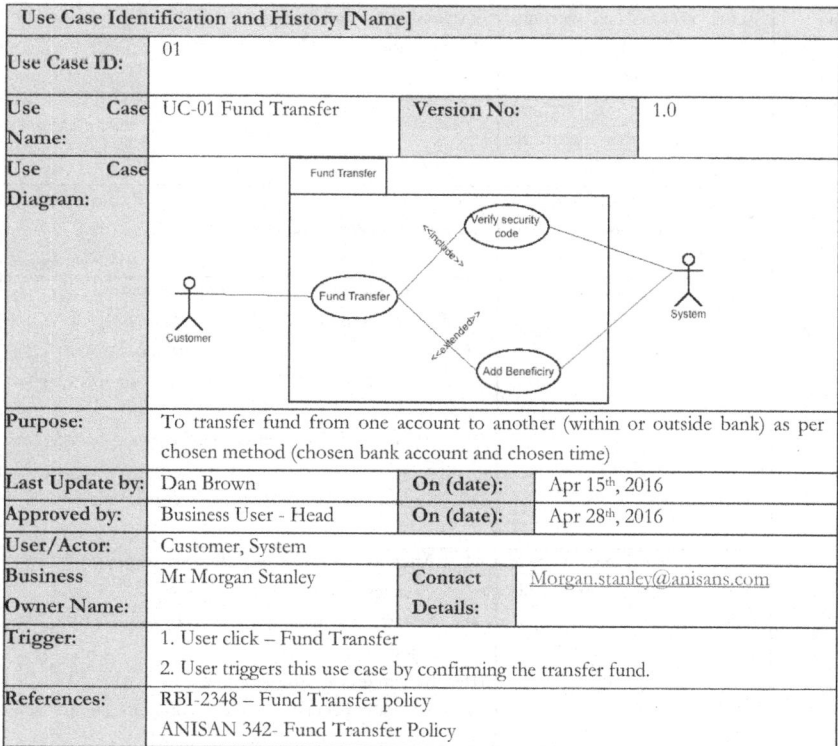		
Purpose:	To transfer fund from one account to another (within or outside bank) as per chosen method (chosen bank account and chosen time)		
Last Update by:	Dan Brown	On (date):	Apr 15th, 2016
Approved by:	Business User - Head	On (date):	Apr 28th, 2016
User/Actor:	Customer, System		
Business Owner Name:	Mr Morgan Stanley	Contact Details:	Morgan.stanley@anisans.com
Trigger:	1. User click – Fund Transfer 2. User triggers this use case by confirming the transfer fund.		
References:	RBI-2348 – Fund Transfer policy ANISAN 342- Fund Transfer Policy		

Frequency of Use:	Often. As and when customer requires transferring the funds.
Preconditions:	1. Actor must be logged on to System 2. The actor must have access rights to transfer the funds, registered mobile number and valid beneficiary in their account.
Post Conditions:	1. Fund is transferred a record created with unique Transfer ID. 2. Accounts are updated 3. Relevant information is distributed in pre-defined structure to the customer.
Non-functional Requirements	At any given time, at least 30,000 customers should be able to transfer the funds.
Assumptions, Issues:	Customer has access to online banking solution. Customer logged into the solution. Customer has beneficiary registered in his account.
Steps:	<<Steps>>

192. What is basic flow?

Basic Flow

Basic Flow		
Step	User Actions	System Response
a.	Actor chooses an account "from" where he desires to transfer the fund.	System displays and prompts for the list of accounts from the repository.
b.	Actor chooses an account "to" where they wish to transfer the fund	System prompts for list of beneficiaries.
c.	Actor specifies the required input (enter amount) in the field.	System checks the data format as integer. If data format is not integer, system prompts the alert.

d.	Confirm the transfer	System provides an option for confirm transfer.
		System verifies business rules:
		  I. Transfer amount less than the balance amount
		  II. Transfer amount less than the daily permissible amount
		  III. After successful verification, System generates the code.
		  IV. System sends the code to the registered mobile

e.	Actor receives security code and enters the security code online.	I. After receiving the security code from user, system validates the same.
		  II. System generate transfer ID and transfer the amount
		  III. System updates the accounts
		  IV. System generates the communication and distribute/send it to the customer.

193. What is alternate flow?
Alternate Flow

Alternate Flow		
Step	User Actions	System Actions
1.	Actor re-enter the amount if amount is not in-line with business rules specified in 4.	System provides an option to re-enter the input and verify again.
2	Actor chooses to use alternate mode of verifying the Security Code.	System provides an option to verify through ATM pin.

194. What is exception flow?
Exception Flow

Exception Flow		
Step	User Actions	System Actions
1	Actor enters bigger amount than the balance amount.	The system throws an alert – There is NO sufficient balance. Please re-enter the amount.
2	Actor is inactive on the system.	The system 'ends the session' for security reason mentioned in FRD no. 2345. The message is displayed – your session has ended. Please re-login.

195. Describe informal or causal version use case.
This is either described in a paragraph using natural language or arranged the through information in a tabular form as shown below.

Overview of the use cases:

You can use a tabular or Excel sheet to present overview of use cases or catalogue to refer:

#	Use Case	Actor	Brief Description	Priority /MoSCoW	Complexity
Unique ID	Name		Brief Description	Business priority (low/med/high/critical) or Ranking them 0-10	Technical complexity (low/med/high) Or Ranking from 0-10
1	Fund Transfer	Customer	Transfer the fund using online banking solution	H	H
2	Add Payee	Customer	Adds payee for the first the payee for transferring the fund	H	M
3	Validate the security code	System	The System generates the security code, send it to the registered mobile and validate same	H	M

196. What are the key points to remember in creating an effective use-case model?

In the case of complex use cases, the business analyst can create two separate models, one for the use case and another for the actor diagram.

Capture the user (person and system) interaction, goal, and the system response to explain how the technology or process functions.

No code is written in modelling. Neither the use case nor the architectural diagram is involved in showing the components and their interaction. The focus remains solely on the user interaction and system response.

Only when the author has all the necessary details to understand, to model, and to document the use case, can he effectively create the use cases.

The author must capture the software system response in the form of a trigger, post-condition, basic flow, alternate flow, exception, business rule, etc.

The user must provide adequate details, as it is the key to creating effective use cases. Too much or too little information will not achieve the goal of explaining it.

To explain the use case, one or two models along with the textual description for each use case are good enough.

Use the template to document use cases. The reader will expect set of information in a structured manner at the predefined place.

Practice it. Review it. Update it. [Cockburn, 2000]

197. What are the differences between an alternate flow and an exception flow of a use case?

"Alternate flow" is an alternate way of achieving the goal that is optional to basic flow. It is required if the basic flow doesn't work to achieve the goal.

Whereas "exception flow" is when an unexpected situation occurs in the form of error. This error could be business or technical error. Invalid data or process or technical error can be caught and informed to the user as well as technical team through a pre-defined message. For example, the 404 error indicates the page is not available online.

198. Provide an example of high-level use case.

The following is an example of a high-level use case diagram. The customer is using login, viewing personal details, and fund transfer functionalities.

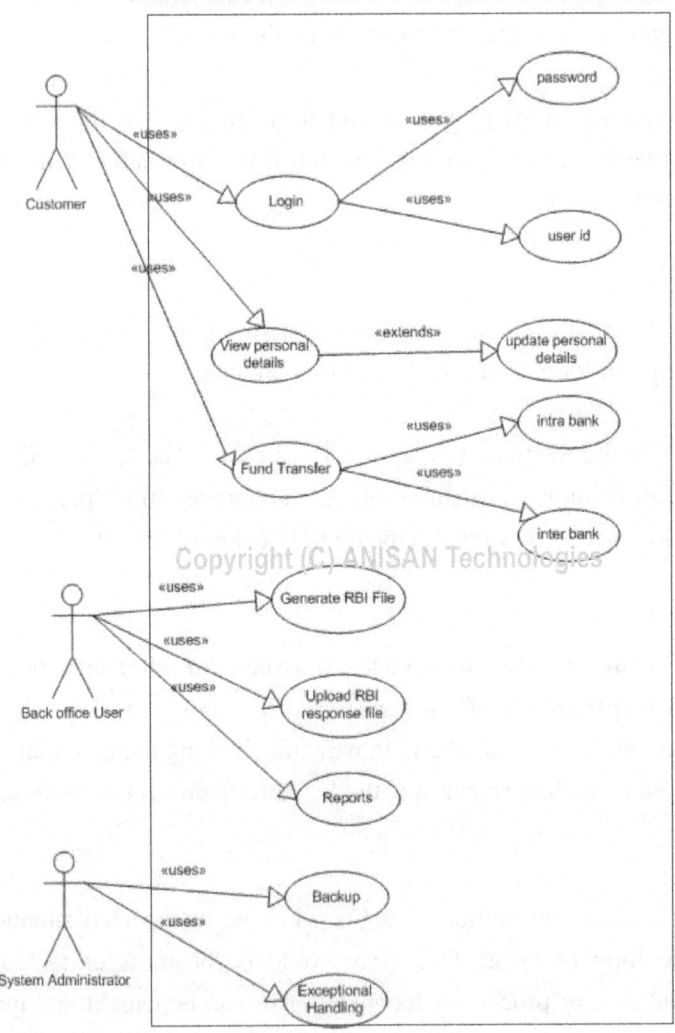

The back-office user generates a RBI (central bank) report file, uploads the same, and generates other report functionalities. The system administrator is using backup and exception handling functionalities.

6.3 Data Modelling

199. What is data modelling?

Data modelling is a system concentrating on the logical entities and dependencies between these entities. It describes the concept related to a domain, system, or solution.

Data modelling is an abstraction of data and database requirements. It emphasizes concepts, people, objects, structure, relationships, name, and data formats of requirements of the systems that are analyzed. It also defines the meaning of the data. [BABOK v2, 2009]

The Entity-Relationship Model or Entity-Relationship Diagram (ERD) or Class Diagram is a data model or diagram for a high-level description of the databases and their relationships. It is a graphical symbolization for representing these models in the form of entity-relationship diagrams. These are typically used in the initial stage of defining the system scope to support the scope and vision document. They are also used for describing information requirements and/or the type of information that is generated and needed during the system life cycle.

Data modelling is used in defining solution scope, defining data requirements, designing databases, defining relationships among data in a context, retrieving data, etc.

200. What is an entity or class or concept?

It is requirement modelling in the data perspective. It describes the entity or concept or class and information associated with it and its relationship (business as well as technical) with another concept or entity or class within the database.

For example, if an employee is an entity or class, the information associated with it would be employee ID, first name, last name, address, city, country, telephone, date of birth and other related details. Every employee will have a unique ID and unique information associated with it. This information is known as a record and stored in a row. The column will represent the attributes and holds information about the specific data of an entity. For example, the data of birth column will have information about data of birth records of all the employees.

Business Definition	Employee ID (primary key)	First Name	Last Name	Address 1	Telephone	Date of Birth	Department (Foreign key)
Database attributes	emp_ID	F_Name	L_Name	add_1	Tel	DOB	Dept_ID
Data Format	Char(5)	varChar(16)	varChar(16)	varChar(16)	Integer (3-3-4)	Date(DD/MM/YY)	varChar(3)
Sample Data	14356	Dan	Brown	123, Main Street, Hong Kong	456-890-4444	01/01/71	S-12

201. What is the difference between an E-R diagram and a Class Diagram?

#	Entity Relationship Diagram	Class Diagram
Used in	Relational database	Objective-oriented database
Concept	Entity	Class
Attributes	Entity Type or Relationship Type or Attributes	Attributes
Operations	Not Applicable	Operations performed on the instances of the class.
Modelling Elements	Cardinality	Multiplicity

Relationship Notations

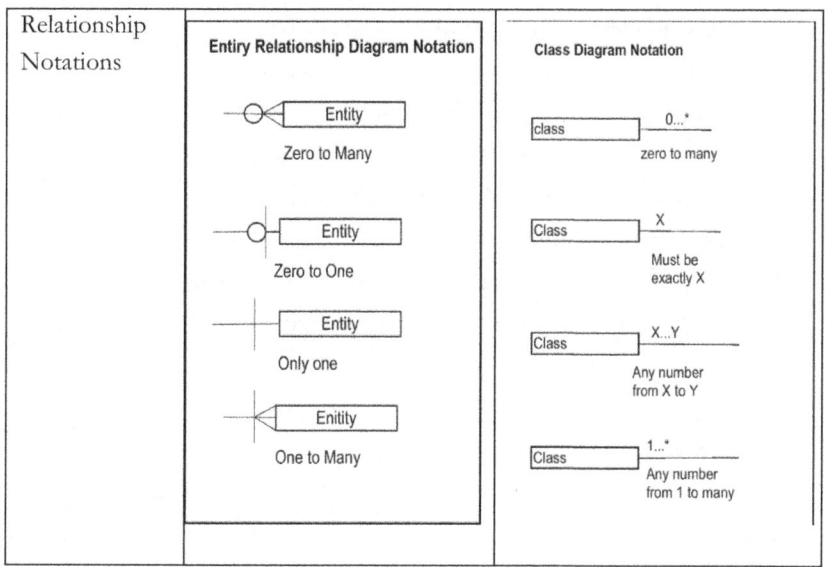

202. What are the different types of association in Class Diagrams?

Notation	Association	Description
──────▶	Association	General Association
── ── ──▶	Inheritance	Parent-child inheritance
── ── ──▷	Realization/ Implementation	One realizes characteristics behavior of source or /supplier
── ── ──▸	Dependency	Uses Part of Source (keyboard is part of computer but is used by other computer)
──────◇	Aggregation	It is an association that represents a part-whole or part-of relationship.
──────◆	Composition	Part of Source (keyboard is part of computer)

a. Association: An association is illustrated with edges.
b. Inheritance: Parent-child relationship where child inherits parent's characteristics
c. Realization/Implementation: One realizes the behaviors of source or parent or supplier model.

d. Dependency: Parent-child relationship where a child is dependent on the parent. A keyboard is dependent on a computer, as it cannot work independently.
e. Aggregation: It is part of the source, but can be used by others. A keyboard is part of a computer. However, it can be used with any other computer.
f. Composition: It is a specific association to denote a part(s). For example, the keyboard is a part of the computer.

203. How to learn SQL concepts.
Please use the following link to practice SQL retrieval queries. Please note that business analysts access the database primarily to verify or analyze or recommend the data. The database team is primarily responsible for updating or modifying the database. In an expectation case, the business analyst may have to modify the database that is rare.

https://www.sqlteaching.com

204. Please describe the data-modelling diagram with an example.
The following diagram depicts data modeling for fund transfer.

Customers, new users, transaction, beneficiary, and charges are "the entities" here and they are logically connected with each other.

6.4 Activity Diagram/Process Diagram

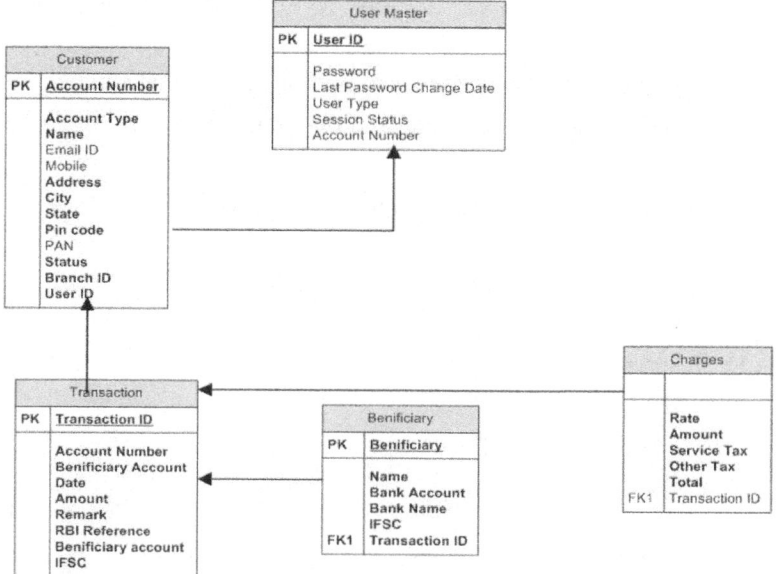

205. What is activity diagram?

The activity diagram is a type of flow chart. Activity diagrams are used to visually model the dynamic behavior of a given part of the system.

They are used to model the dynamic behavior of a number of elements of an object-oriented system and also used to model use cases. [Windle, Abreo, 2003]

206. What are flowcharts and why are they used?

Flow charts provide the visual summary of the software solution through standard symbols, notations, text, and diagrams to bring the readers on the same understanding level by providing required clarity. This also removes any interpretation or communication gaps mentioned in the documents.

207. What are the major elements in an activity diagram?

The following are the activity diagram notations.

The first row illustrates the name of the activity, start, and end node.

The second row shows the various control flow that can be used and third row shows the decision node and merge node.

The forth row depicts the synchronization bar – fork or join.

The last row describes the hierarchization within the activity diagram.

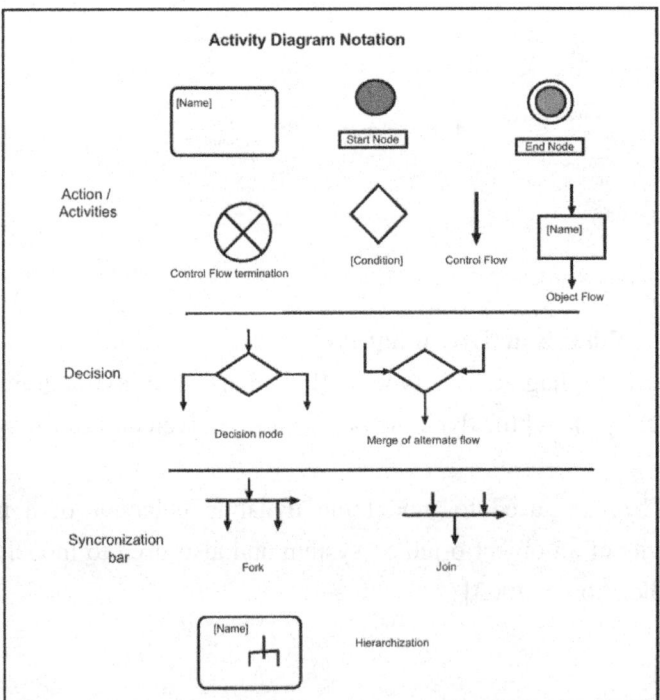

Initial Node:

The initial node is a control node at which flow begins when the activity is invoked.

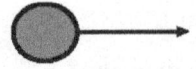

Start node or Initial node

A control token is in place at the initial node or when the activity starts. Until the activity starts, the node is in a passive state. For example, an ATM machine is activated when a customer inserts the bankcard.

A token in an initial node is offered one or more outgoing edges. For example, the customer is advised multiple choices/services once he authenticates user credentials. However, those options or services are blocked if the customer fails to authenticate the account credentials. In this manner, initial nodes are an exception to the rule that controls the nodes.

For convenience, initial nodes are an exception to the rule that controls the nodes.

There may be other opening nodes in the diagram, especially those that lead to an activity. Therefore, the initial node is necessary only in the early stage. To differentiate the initial node from other start-flow nodes within the activity, the former is depicted as a solid circle and other nodes are not. Instead, they are represented as small circles.

Control Flow Termination Node:

Flow End node or Final node

The final node is a control that halts a flow.

Similar to the initial nodes, the final nodes may have more than one final node.

It is depicted by a small circle with an "X" symbol inside.

Please note that there is no impact on other flows in the activity.

For example, in an ATM (automatic teller machine) operation, a customer can choose to withdraw cash. Once the cash withdrawal is complete, that flow is concluded. The ATM may offer other flows such as check the balance or transfer money. However, customer may also have an option to terminate the main activity by selecting "Exit".

Activity Final Node:

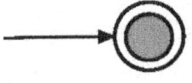

Activity final node is a final terminating point where all flows within the activity end.

Activity End node or Final node

One or more flow will terminate at this stage and a circle within the circle illustrates this node. The inner circle is solid and filled with red color.

For example, in an ATM, the final stage is when a customer completes the interaction and selects "exit". At this stage, the customer receives the card and cash if he has chosen to withdraw it, and a receipt for the transaction.

Control Flow: An arrowed line is used to denote Control Flow that connects two actions or flow.

Control or Decision: It is used for depicting the decision.
A diamond shape is used to control the flow.
Action and Object Control
Fork Node, Join Node, and Combined Fork Node, and Join Node:

Action and Object Control

Fork Node	Join Node	Combined Fork Node and Join Node
"A ForkNode is a control node that distributes single flow into multiple edges. This will	"A JoinNode is a control node that synchronizes multiple edges. This will have	It is combined JoinNode and a ForkNode that has multiple incoming ActivityEdges and

have a single incoming edges and multiple outgoing ActivityEdges."	multiple incoming edges and one outgoing ActivityEdge."	multiple outgoing ActivityEdges.
![fork]	![decision]	![fork-join]
If incoming nodes are ObjectFlows, the outgoing nodes will be ObjectFlows; else they will be ControlFlows.		

If incoming nodes are ObjectFlows, the outgoing nodes will be ObjectFlows; else they will be ControlFlows.

(OMG, 2002]

208. Provide an example of an activity diagram.

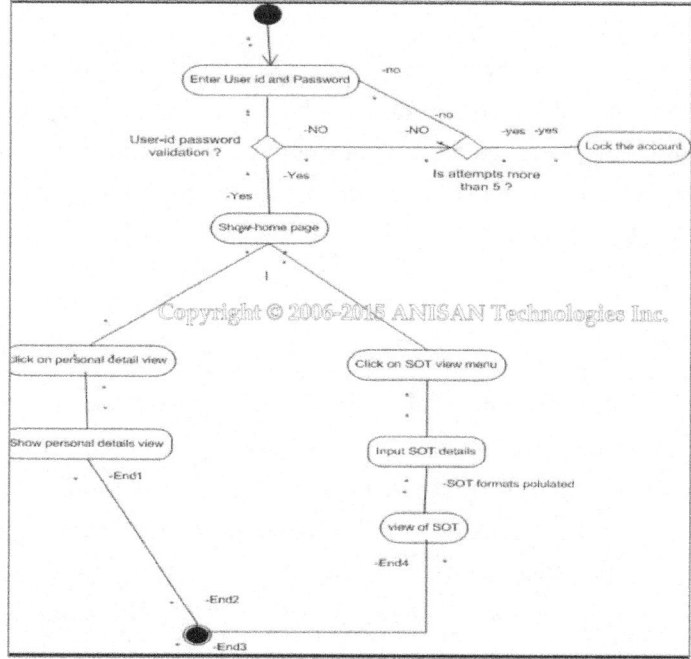

The following activity diagram depicts the personal banking activities performed by users. These activities include the login process, view menu, view personal details, view statement of transaction (SOT) in various formats, etc.

209. What is a process diagram?

A process diagram is a graphical representation of the process. It is a well-defined series of activities designed to achieve a particular goal. The goal could be ordering an item from an online store, fixing a broken part in a machine, delivering a good or service or cooking a recipe.

These process diagrams can use various standards such as BPMN or UML.

A process contains a starting point and an endpoint, also known as start and end events respectively. [kossak, Illibauer et el, 2015]

210. How to build a simple Process Architecture?

Step 1: Name the Processes

Starting with the current state, have stakeholders name in-scope processes using the form "[Somebody] [does something] [with/to something]." For example, a customer purchases an item or order for a service from the company. Write these on the sticky-notes and stick them on the whiteboard.

Step 2: Arrange the Processes

i) Move an important process (A) to an open area on the whiteboard.
ii) Find a process (B) that depends on A, or that A depends on. If B depends on A, stick B below A. If A depends on B, stick B above A.
iii) Draw a line between A and B. Note the nature of the relationship with a short statement. A manager performing

"credit check" will depend on the salesperson assisting the customer in the showroom. The relationship could be labeled if the customer decides to buy an item.

Repeat the activities until all processes are related. You may discover new processes or merge some. Space out the sticky-notes and look for relationships between processes that are already arranged, e.g., two processes that require access to the same machine, so they can't happen simultaneously.

Step 3: Identify Additional Actors
Each process name states at least one actor. Also, note other actors on the sticky-note. For example, a manager performing customer credit checks needs a customer, credit bureau and sales tracking system.

Step 4: Identify Information Flows
Note information that must be exchanged between processes as inputs and outputs. Keep it simple. For instance, if customer information is enough, don't list first name, last name, eye color, etc.

Step 5: Define External Inputs and Outputs
Draw a line around all in-scope processes. Some of these have relationships with out-of-scope processes. Define these by following steps from 1 to 4, replacing "in-scope" with "out-of-scope".

Step 6: Document Take a picture of the raw process architecture for translation into another form (MS-Vision or any similar tool to draw the process diagram).

Step 7: Future State
Adjust the model with a new color, showing the changes that will be applied to the processes and relationships during the project.

The customer submits the funds transfer request at the front office.

The front office officer verifies the "Funds Transfer" request with respect to its validity and completeness. If everything is in order, the front office officer acknowledges and provides the receipt.

Based on the type of funds transfer, an appropriate entry is made in the Central Bank System (CBS).

In the case of intra-bank fund transfers, the respective accounting entry is passed, and the money is transferred instantly.

In the case of inter-bank funds transfers, the fund transfer details are captured and verified with the Central Bank System (CBS).

Based on the type of inter-bank transfer, the respective file is generated to upload to the central bank or clearing-house.

The central bank processes fund transfer request and generates a response file for the bank.

The response file from the central bank is updated in the Central Bank System and respective credits/debits are reflected in the customer's accounts.

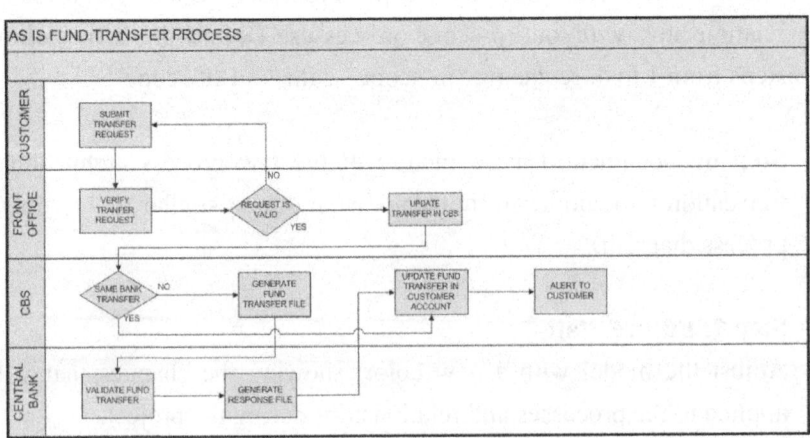

6.5 State Diagram

211. What is a state diagram?

UML state diagram or state diagram machine, or state chart are used to capture the distinct behavior of the component of the designed system through finite state transition. There are two types of state diagrams. Mealy (1955) defined that the output of automation depends on the current state of the automation as well as on the input. Meanwhile, Moor Autmata (1956) opined that output was dependent on the current state.

Most modern analysts and UML (uml.org) use Harrel (1987) concept of state diagram that is based on finite-state automata and support the hierarchization of the states to document condition of the state transitions and to model concurrent behavior, thus making them more reactive in nature. A state defines a particular state of the system and depicts specific behavior in that state.

212. What are the state diagram notations?

    a. Initial State: It describes a state when a system is ideal and waiting for user inputs. It is also known as a default state or composite state. It is depicted with a small solid circle.

    b. Final State: It is a state that describes when a system completes its process and is awaiting the next cycle. Thus, it could be returning to the initial state. It is depicted by a circle and cross (to indicate stop). For example, the ATM machine initial state and final state is the same after the user or customer completes the transaction. When it completes the cycle, it goes back to the initial state and is ready for a new transaction-cycle.

    c. Entry Point: It is an entry point of state or composite state. It is depicted by a small circle on the border of the state.

d. Exit Point: It is an "exit" point of a state machine or state chart diagram. It implies exit of the state by sub-state, or composite state, or submachine sate, and triggers of the transition, which has this as an "exit point" as basis in the state machine enfolding the submachine or composite state.

e. Fork: A fork notation in a UML activity and state diagram is a control node that splits a flow into multiple concurrent flows or state. This will have one incoming edge and multiple outgoing flows or edges.

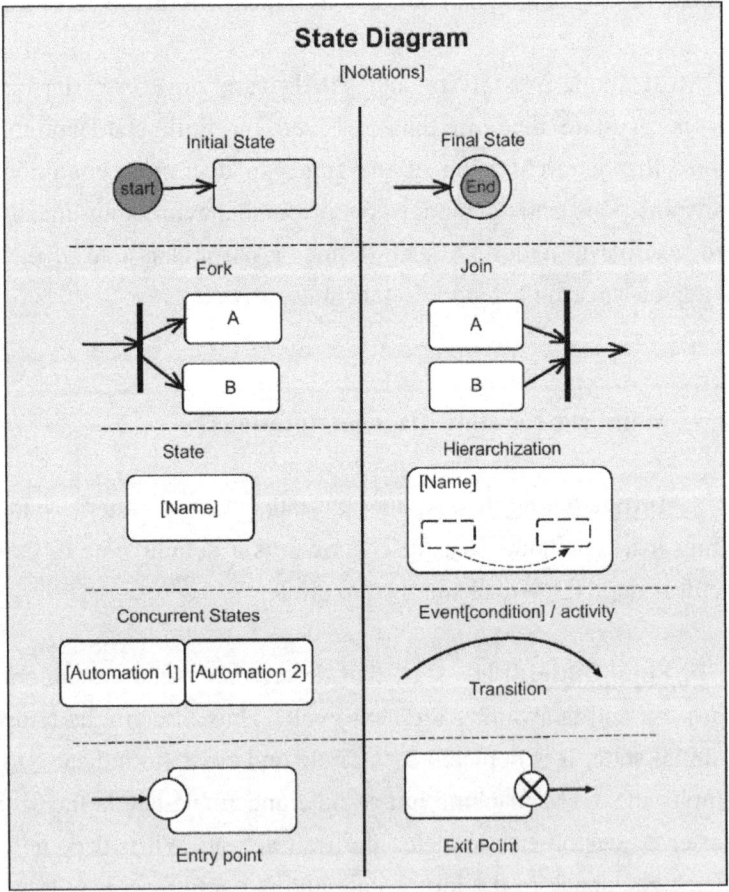

f. Join: It is a control node that synchronizes multiple flows or states. This will have multiple incoming edges and one outgoing edge.

g. State: It defines a period of time in which the system exhibits a specific behavior.

h. Hierarchization: it is a hierarchical refinement of states that in turn represents automata. The initial state is known at a super state and it is defined by a number of refining states.

i. Concurrent States: This represents two or more concurrent automata. It can be a result of decomposition of hierarchization or it can be synchronized through transition condition.

j. Transition: It is a particular state that is triggered by a certain event. [Harel 1988]

213. Please provide state diagram description.
The below-mentioned state diagram shows the behavior of the Café Order System Initially, the system is in the state ''IDLE/start menu''. By touching the "IDLE/start" screen, the system enters into the "super state", and within the "super state", into the sub-state "SELECT [Pasta, Pizza]" and subsequently another sub-state "SELECT OPTION" by making use of entry point "SELECT OPTION". After selecting the option for Pasta or Pizza, the system provides an additional optional action for adding a beverage before 'CONFIRM [order]' mode.

Alternatively, the system changes from the state "IDLE" to "SELECT [Juice or Coffee]" of super state Café Order System into the internal state by making use of "entry point", 'beverage selection' occurs. Once the Café Order System is active: "SELECT the beverage", after the CONFIRM, the system enters into "CONFIRM [order]" mode.

Once the "CONFIRM [order]" event occurs, the system offers "SELECT payment mode", upon successfully validating the payment, the system transitions into Order Complete via PRINT receipt and re-enter or transition into state Café Order System "IDLE/Start Menu".

If any cancellation is received, the system is transitioned into the state "IDLE/Start Menu" once the event "cancel" occurs.

If the system is in the state Café Order System PRINT receipt and order is completed successfully, the system exits the super state Café Order System via the system exit point.

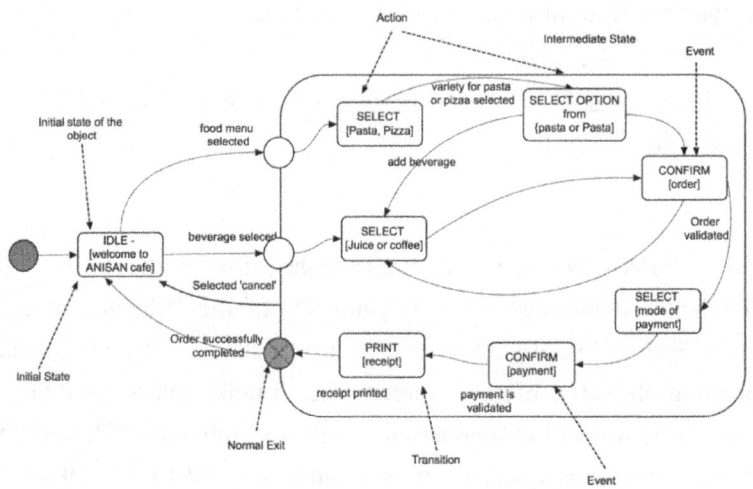

State Diagram: Cafe Order System

Food order system state diagram model

Model sub-states or hierarchy of the state machine for Café Order System. Top-level state machines have initial and final states. The diagram shows the collection of sub-states (SELECT MENU, SELECT SUB-MENU, SELECT OPTION TO ADD, CONFIRM, SELECT PAYMENT and PRINT RECEIPT of the Café Order System also known "super-state."

CONFIRM PAYMENT is a sub-state of transitions, and PRINT RECEIPT confirms the completion of the order, i.e., the super-state.

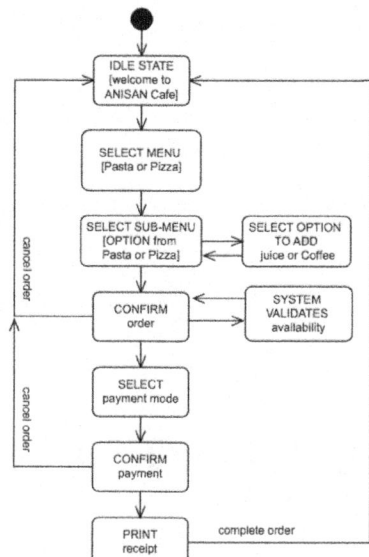

State Diagram: Cafe Order System

7 Disposition

"And I realized that there's a big difference between deciding to leave and knowing where to go."
— *Robyn Schneider, The Beginning of Everything*

"Ends are not bad things, they just mean that something else is about to begin. And there are many things that don't really end, anyway, they just begin again in a new way. Ends are not bad and many ends aren't really an ending; some things are never-ending."
— *C. JoyBell C.*

214. What is the decommissioning process?

It is orderly termination or disposition of the software system when it reaches to the end of its life cycle.

There are various business and technical reasons for decommissioning, including discontinuation of the products, or services, outdated business model, lack of a sponsor to support, outmoded technology, and migration to the existing application to curtail redundancy. In addition, if the service or system is a drain on funds or contributing to creating a negative perception of the brand or company image, the management may decide to decommission the service and associated system.

215. Explain in detail what is the decommissioning process.

It requires fulfilling organizational, local, and federal standards to preserve important data, information, and documentations. The preserved data may be utilized if needed in the future and can be easily retrieved. So, the data must be organized and structure before being archived. Proper planning is required for structuring, storing, accessing, and documenting. The storage of the data must be done as per the organization's information management system regulations and policies.

Decommissioning, therefore, implies orderly termination activity conducted through the following process:
  a) Proposal
  b) Planning and approval
  c) Resource allocation
  d) Discontinuity of business
  e) Deactivation of IT service/system,
  f) Preservation and management of vital data about the system
  g) Disposal of unwanted data, hardware, and software.

a. Proposal:

The business analyst, along with stakeholder and project manager, will assess the need of decommissioning the service or system and prepare the proposal.

b. Planning for approval:
It is a planning for the disposition process. Identify resources and their role in the disposition process. In this case, the resources include stakeholders who will participate and their nature of participation and resources such as software, hardware, network, or other infrastructure that is required to be released pre-and post-disposition.

c. Resource allocation:
This process includes allocating the work to relevant resources.

It means an orderly termination process and related activities are assigned to relevant stakeholders. For example, informing customers about discontinuation of the services well in advance and providing them alternate options. Also, communicating with the database team to take the backup as specified in the disposition requirements.

d. Discontinuation of business services:
Before the discontinuity process starts, the person responsible for communication needs to inform all the relevant users and stakeholders about the system going offline and future steps that need to be taken before and after service or system or solution goes offline.

The types of actions that will be initiated, executed, and completed are categorized based on the user role.

e. Revisit business case
The business analyst must perform a return on investment (ROI) to validate the estimated business case against the actual business case.

f. Deactivation of services and systems

Identify the activities involved in deactivating the services, i.e., deactivate from users and arrange new services or system in the user community. This is to ensure smooth transition of new services or systems in the user community, removal of the services or systems from the user community or production environment, taking the backup of data if the old system is discontinued and documenting the details of the storage.

g. Preservation and record management:
The purpose of preservation of data through storage and record management is to be able to access some or all of the information that may be used in the future.

Data in the form of requirements, business rules, references, master data or other details are stored in the project library for future use.

h. Completion of decommissioning:
Decommissioning is completed when the resources are handed over to the stakeholders. These resources include database, records, access details, etc., that are obtained after getting a sign-off from authorized signatories. [Calero, Piattini, 2013]

8 Essentials of Business Analysis

"Few things are impossible to diligence and skill. Great works are performed not by strength, but by perseverance."
— *Samuel Johnson*

8.1 Types Of Testing

216. What are the types of testing? Describe each type in details.
- Independent verification and validation
- Configuration control
- Integration
- User Documentation
- Unit testing
- Function Testing
- Regression testing
- Integration testing
- Performance testing
- Security testing
- Usability testing
- System testing
- Cloud testing
- Field (beta) testing
- Acceptance testing
- Independent testing

The detailed descriptions of these types of testing are provided in next questions.

217. What is Integration testing?

Objective: The integration test is conducted to verify that the combined parts of an application function together correctly. Any application is made up of smaller units called modules, which interact with each other via API's or interfaces. Also, integration testing on a larger scale involves testing of integration of one system with another system and validating the communication between them.

The techniques:
- Integration testing is done by using three approaches:

- o a. Big bang,
- o b. Bottom-up, and
- o c. Top-down.
- In each technique, modules are integrated with each other level wise either top to down or bottom to up.

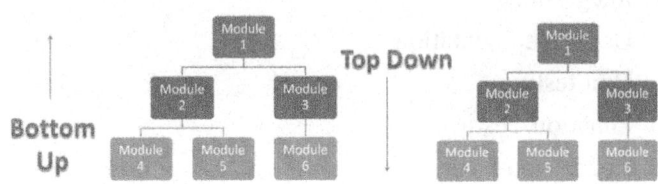

What is to be tested?
- User interface interaction (GUI) with the application databases like Oracle or MySQL or MS SQL Server, etc.
- All interaction with other applications (feeds into and out of the system)
- Examples of application testing involve testing various features the application provides. Testing of sending out an email, deleting an email, storing an email in drafts folder, etc. in MS Outlook can be considered as application testing. Each of these features is a module, and when integrated together, they form an application.
- System-to-system integration and testing of communication between them.
- Validating job execution (proper triggering of jobs in flow and out flow)
- Manually checking the database for accuracy
- Manually checking for notification messages on GUI
- Validation of all generated reports after the integration has been accomplished.

Success criteria: Successful interaction of the modules in the application and successful interaction of various systems communicating with each other.

Example: Testing of features in MS Outlook like sending an email, deleting an email, composing an email, etc. All these modules integrate to form an application. Testing of all these modules integrated together is known as integration testing.

218. What is User Interface testing?

Test Objective:

The user interface testing is performed to validate whether the Graphical User Interface (GUI) of the application is functioning as specified. For example, navigation through the target-of-test properly reflects business functions and requirements, including window-to-window (user screens), field-to-field, and use of access methods (tab keys, mouse movements, accelerator keys, etc.).

Also validate the window objects and characteristics, such as menu(s), size, position, state, and focus conforming to standards. GUI testing has gained a lot of importance in today's world where all the web and mobile apps are highly user-centric. Another important aspect of GUI testing is user experience. Testing should be focused on validating whether the screens match up the wire frames provided by the client and also ensure that the developed UI is easy to use for the end user.

The techniques:

Create or modify tests for each window to verify proper navigation and object states for each application window and objects. "State Transition Testing" should be performed to ensure the navigation flow from one page to another (back and forth). Test cases should focus on testing each and every component that would be visible on the screen to the end user. Utmost care should be taken to ensure all the hyperlinks on the web page redirect to the designated destination.

Success criteria:

This involves successfully verification of each window to remain consistent with the benchmark version or within an acceptable standard.

Special consideration: Not all properties for the custom and third-party objects can be accessed.

Example: Navigate to any site such as 'amazon.com'. When you visit this web site, you look out for various controls, menus, displays, fonts, colors, navigation to web pages etc., which are part of the "look and feel" requirements. Testing of these as per the wireframes provided by the clients and validating the exact requirement is called as GUI testing.

219. What is Function testing?
Test Objective:
Ensure proper target-of-test functionality, including navigation, data entry, processing, and retrieval. Functional testing should focus on validating whether the built-in application intends to do what it is meant for. Expected result and actual results should be logged and compared with each other to ensure that there is no discrepancy in the application developed.

Technique:
- Execute each use case, use case flow, or function, using valid and invalid data to verify the following:
- The expected results occur when valid data is used.
- Test the corner cases and validate how the application reacts to the inputted data.
- The appropriate error or warning messages are displayed when invalid data is used.
- Each business rule is properly applied.
- Various functional testing techniques can be applied for performing it, viz:
    - Unit Testing
    - Smoke Testing
    - Sanity Testing

- Integration Testing
- White box testing
- Black Box testing
- User Acceptance testing
- Regression Testing

Success Criteria:
- All planned tests have been executed by using various testing techniques
- All identified defects have been identified, logged, and reported.

220. What is Data Integrity testing?

Test Objective:
To ensure accuracy and consistency of the database, as well as access methods and processes, and proper functioning without the data is getting corrupted. Data integrity testing should verify data in the database is accurate and functions in line with the application.

Technique:
- Invoke each database access method and process, using each with valid as well as invalid data (or requests for data).
- Inspect the database to ensure the data has been populated as planned. Also, check if all database events occurred properly, and verify the returned data to ensure that the correct data is retrieved (for the precise reasons).

Completion Criteria:
- All database access methods and processes function as designed and without any data corruption.

Special Considerations:
- A DBMS development environment or drivers required for entering or modifying data directly in the databases.

- Processes should be manually invoked. A sample size of small records or database (limited number of records) can be used to increase the visibility of any non-acceptable events

221. What is Security and Access Control testing?

Test Objective:
Application-level security: It is to verify that an actor can access only the permissible functions or data for which approval is granted for his user type.

System-level security: It is to verify that only those actors having access to the system and application(s) are approved to access them.

Technique:
Application-level: Identify and list each actor type and the functions/data each type has permissions for. Test the authentication and authorization for each role and validate whether the user can access only the designated part of the application.

- Test the admin login for authorization and granting access to the list of users.
- Create the tests for each actor type to verify each permission by setting up the transactions especially for each user actor.
- Modify user type and re-run tests for the same users. In each case, verify whether those additional functions or data are available or denied correctly.

    System-level Access (See particular considerations below)

Completion Criteria:
This is to verify that the appropriate function or data are available for each identified actor type, and all the transaction functions run as expected.

Special Considerations:

This is to verify that the access to the system is reviewed and communicated to the appropriate network or systems administrator. This testing may not be required as it may be a function of network or systems administration.

222. What is Usability testing?

Test Objective:

To verify that the application design fully integrates with the user's business processes, giving the user of the application a smooth and seamless flow through the application while performing their job. The main focus of usability testing should be on ease of using the application and whether it fulfills the end users' requirements.

Technique:

- One-on-one interaction of a business user with a usability engineer.
- Encouraging user input as they work with the application.
- Recording user's nonverbal activity while using the application.
- Always questioning the business user for the feedback on navigation, screen design, screen content, etc.
- Recording the user experience and non-functional aspects such as ease of use, performance of the application etc.

Completion Criteria:

- The application is complete and intuitive to the user.
- System navigation is consistent with the business user's workflow.
- Training is minimized due to a good intuitive design.

223. What are Fail Over and Recovery testing?

Test Objective: To verify that recovery processes (manual or automated) properly restore the database, applications, and system to a desired or

known state. The following types of conditions are to be included in the testing:
- Power interruption to the client
- Power interruption to the server
- Communication interruption via network server(s)
- Interruption, communication, or power loss to DASD and or DASD controller(s)
- Incomplete cycles (interruption of data filter and data synchronization processes)
- Invalid database pointer or keys invalid or corrupted data element in database

Technique:
Tests created for function and business cycle testing should be used to create a series of transactions. Once the desired starting test point is reached, the following actions should be individually performed or simulated individually:

- Power interruption to the client: Power the PC down
- Power interruption to the server: Simulate or initiate power down procedures for the server

Interruption via network servers: Simulate or initiate communication loss with the network (physically disconnects communication wires or power down network server(s) or routers).

Interruption, communication, or power loss to DASD and or DASD controller(s): Simulate or physically eliminate communication with one or more DASD controllers or devices.

Once the above conditions or simulated conditions are achieved, additional transactions should be executed, and upon reaching this second test point state, recovery procedures should be invoked.

Testing for incomplete cycles utilizes the same technique as described above except that the database processes themselves should be aborted or prematurely terminated.

Testing for the following conditions requires that a known database state to be achieved. Several database fields, pointers, and keys should be corrupted manually and directly within the database (via database tools). Database checkpoints should be added. When the failure occurs, it should be validated that the transaction has been rolled back to the checkpoint. Additional transactions should be executed using the tests from application function and business cycle testing and full cycles executed.

Completion Criteria:
In all of the cases above, the application, database, and system should, upon completion of recovery procedures, will return to a known or desirable state. This state includes data corruption limited to the known corrupted fields, pointers/keys, and reports indicating the processes or transactions that were not completed due to interruptions.

Special Considerations:
Recovery testing is highly intrusive. Procedures to disconnect cabling (simulating power or communication loss) may not be desirable or feasible. Alternative methods, such as diagnostic software tools, may be required.

Resources from the systems (or computer operations), database, and networking groups are required.

These tests should either be run after hours or on an isolated machine(s).

224. **What is Performance Profiling testing?**

Test Objective:
To verify performance behaviors for designated transactions or business functions under the following conditions:
- Normal anticipated workload
- Anticipated worst-case workload

Technique:
Use test procedures developed for function or business cycle testing.
- Modify data files (to increase the number of transactions) or the scripts to increase the number of iterations.
- Scripts should be run on one machine (best case to benchmark single user or single transaction) and be repeated with multiple clients (virtual or actual, see special considerations below).

Note the turnaround time for the transaction and validate it with the expected result.

Completion Criteria:
Single transaction/single user: Successful completion of the test scripts without any failures and within the expected/required time allocation (per transaction)

Multiple transactions / multiple users: Successful completion of the test scripts without any failures and within acceptable time allocation.

Special Considerations: Comprehensive performance testing includes having a "background" workload on the server.

There are several methods that can be used to perform this, including:

- "Drive transactions" directly to the server, usually in the form of SQL calls.
- Create a "virtual" user load to simulate many (usually several hundred) clients. Remote terminal emulation tools are used to

accomplish this load. This technique can also be used to load the network with "traffic."
- Use multiple physical clients, each running test scripts to place a load on the system.

Performance testing should be performed on a dedicated machine or at a dedicated time. This permits full control and accurate measurement.

The databases used for performance testing should be either actual size, or scaled equally.

Application specific testing:
The online banking application must be tested under the following conditions in order to certify performance response times:
- Connected to the network
- Not connected to the network (connected directly to the server)
- If response times are in question, this testing will define if the problem is in the application code or on the network. The "network" test will be conducted in a remote planner's office (i.e., New York) while the "not connected to the network" test will be conducted at the location of the host server.
- The performance metrics will be tested as per the requirements. These metrics will include transaction rates, uptime/downtime screen refresh rate, etc.

The online banking application must also be tested online as well as off-line. Using a PC configured with the minimum acceptable hardware requirements (as defined in the online banking – Release one business requirements document) the application will be tested both online and off-line to assure response times are compliant with the business requirements.

225. What is Load testing?
Test Objective:

To verify performance behaviors' time for designated transactions or business cases under varying workload conditions.

Technique:
Use tests developed for function or business cycle testing.
   Modify data files (to increase the number of transactions) or the tests to increase the number of times each transaction occurs.

   Note the maximum load/transactions the system can handle and test it to validate the breakpoint/failure point.

Completion Criteria: Multiple transactions/multiple users: Successful completion of the tests without any failures and within an acceptable time allocation.

Special Considerations:
Load testing should be performed on a dedicated machine or at a dedicated time. This permits full control and accurate measurement.

   The databases used for load testing should be either actual size or scaled equally.

226. What is Stress testing?
Test Objective:
Verify that the target-of-test functions properly and without error under the following stress conditions:
- Little or no memory available on the server (RAM and DASD)
- More than the designated number of users (actual or physically capable) connected to the system (or simulated)
- Multiple users performing the same transactions against the same data/accounts
- Worst-case transaction volume/mix (see performance testing above).

Note: The goal of a stress test might also be stated as identify and document the conditions under which the system FAILS to continue functioning properly.

Stress testing of the client is described under the section on configuration testing.

Technique:
Use tests developed for performance profiling or load testing.

To test limited resources, a test should be run on single machine and RAM and DASD on a server should be reduced (or limited).

For remaining stress tests, multiple clients should be used, either running the same tests or complementary tests to produce the worst-case transaction volume/mix.

Completion Criteria:
All planned tests are executed and specified system limits are reached/exceeded, without the software or software failing (or conditions under which system failure occurs is outside of the specified conditions).

Special Considerations:
Stressing the network may require network deployment of tools to load the network with messages/packets.

The DASD used for the system should temporarily be reduced to restrict the available space for the database to grow.

Also, test the synchronization of the simultaneous clients accessing of the same records or data accounts.

227. What is Volume testing?
Test Objective:
To verify that the target-of-test successfully functions under the following high-volume scenarios:

- Maximum (actual or physically capable) number of clients connected (or simulated) all performing the same, worst-case (performance) business function for an extended period.
- Maximum database size has been reached (actual or scaled) and multiple queries or report transactions are executed simultaneously.

Technique:
Use tests developed for performance profiling or load testing.
- Multiple clients should be used, either running the same tests or complementary tests to produce the worst-case transaction volume/mix (see stress test above) for an extended period.
- Maximum database size is created (actual, scaled, or filled with representative data) and multiple clients are used to run queries / report transactions simultaneously for extended periods.

Completion Criteria:
All planned tests have been executed, and specified system limits are reached/exceeded without the software or software failing.

Special Considerations:
What is a time period would be considered as acceptable for high volume conditions (as noted above)?

228. What is configuration testing?

Test Objective:
To verify that the target-of-test functions properly on the required hardware/software configurations.

Technique:
Use function test scripts.

- Open/close various non-target-of-test related software, such as the Microsoft applications, Excel and Word, either as part of the test or prior to the start of the test.
- Execute selected transactions to simulate actor's interacting with the target-of-test and the non-target-of-test software
- Repeat the above process, minimizing the available conventional memory to the client.

Completion Criteria:
For each combination of the target-of-test and non-target-of-test software, all transactions are successfully completed without failure.

Special Considerations:
What non-target-of-test software is available or accessible on the desktop?

What are typical applications used?

What data are the applications running (i.e., a large spreadsheet opened in Excel or 100-page document in Word)?

The entire systems, NetWare, network servers, databases, etc. should also be documented as part of this test.

229. What is installation testing?
Test Objective:
Verify that the target-of-test correctly installs onto each required hardware configuration, under the following conditions (as required):

- New installation, a new machine, never installed previously with [software].
- Update computer that has previously installed software with the same version

- Update computer that has previously installed software with older version

Technique:
Either manually or develop automated scripts to validate the condition of the target machine [new software] never installed, [software] same version or older version already installed.

- Launch or perform installation.

Using a predetermined sub-set of function test scripts to run the transactions.

Completion Criteria: [Software] Transactions executed successfully without failure.

Special Considerations:
What [software] transactions should be selected to comprise a confidence test so that [software] application could be successfully installed without missing any major software components?

230. What is Business Cycle testing?
Test Objective:
Ensure proper target-of-test and background processes function according to required business models and schedules.

Technique:
Testing will simulate several business cycles by performing the following:

The tests used for the target-of-test's function testing will be modified or enhanced to increase the number of times each function is executed to simulate several different users over a specified period.

- All time or date sensitive functions will be executed using valid and invalid dates or time periods.
- All functions that occur on a periodic schedule will be executed or launched at the appropriate time.
- Testing will include using valid and invalid data, to verify the following:
    o The expected results occur when valid data is used.
- The appropriate error or warning messages are displayed when invalid data is used.
- Each business rule is correctly applied.

Completion Criteria:
- All planned tests have been executed.
- All identified defects have been addressed.

Special Considerations:
System dates and events may require special support activities

A business model is required to identify appropriate test requirements and procedures.

8.2 Sample Test Case

231. Describe the Sample Test Case in informal and formal way.

Example 1:

Test ID	123
Title	Login Module
Test Steps	1. Open Internet Explorer and navigate to www.anisans.com 2. Enter the "User ID" in the Username field 3. Enter "Password" in the Password field 4. Click on the "Login" button

Expected Result	Positive Testing
	
	   Correct User ID + Password
	
	   You are logged into the system
	
	Negative Testing for incorrect User ID/Password
	
	The message is displayed in red font – Login Failed due to incorrect user ID/password. Please re-enter.

Test Result	Passed/Failed

Example 2:

Test Case ID:	Test Case Name	
		06-Jun-18
Test Design ID:		

Test items:

Identify and briefly describe the items and features to be exercised by this test case. For each item, consider supplying references to the following test item documentation:

a) Requirements specification:
b) Design specification:
c) Users guide:
d) Operations guide:
e) Installation guide:

Input specifications:	Specify each input required to execute the test case. Some of the inputs will be specified by value (with tolerances where appropriate), while others, such as constant tables or transaction files, will be specified by name. Identify all appropriate databases, files, terminal messages, memory resident areas, and values passed by the operating system. Specify all required relationships between inputs (e.g., timing).
Output specifications: **(Expected Result)**	Specify all of the outputs and features (e.g., response time) required of the test items. Provide the exact value (with tolerances where appropriate) for each required output or feature.
Actual Result:	Log the actual result, which you got after running the tests.
Environmental needs:	Test Environment Details: Example SIT Server 2 with build #4109 deployed Database Connection: Database name with latest patch applied version. Hardware: Specify the characteristics and configurations of the hardware required to execute this test case (e.g., 132 characters, 24-line CRT). Software: Specify the system and application software required to execute this test case. This may include system software such as operating systems, compilers, simulators, and test tools. In addition, the test item may interact with application software. Other: Specify any other requirements such as unique facility needs or specially trained personnel.

[IEEE, 1998]

8.3 User Acceptance Testing

232. Provide Sample User Acceptance Testing template.

UAT SAMPLE AND RESULT DOCUMENT

GLOBAL BANK LTD- ONLINE BANKING SOLUTION (Built Version 1.1)

Copyright © 2004-2012 ANSAN Technologies Inc.

Test Number	Use Case Number	Functionality	Test Condition	Steps	Expected Result	Actual Result	Test Pass/Fail	Criticality
TC_001	USCA_011	Fund Transfer	Registration of Beneficiary account	1. Login 2. Click link for Fund Transfer 3. Click on link for Beneficiary account registration 3. Fill the information and submit the details such as IFSC, Bank Account etc.	Beneficiary account should be registered	Beneficiary account is registered	pass	-
TC_002	USCA-012	Fund Transfer	Fund Transfer Transaction - Intra Bank	1. Login 2. Click link for Fund Transfer 3. Select fund transfer type as Intra Bank 3. Select Beneficiary account 4. Capture amount, remarks etc. 5. Submit and Confirm the	Customer account should be debited and beneficiary account should be credited	Customer account should is debited and beneficiary account should is credited	pass	-
TC_003	USCA-012	Fund Transfer	Fund Transfer Transaction - Inter Bank	1. Login 2. Click link for Fund Transfer 3. Select fund transfer type as Inter Bank 3. Select transfer type 4. Select Beneficiary account 4. Capture amount, remarks etc. 5. Submit and Confirm the	Customer account should be debited and the transfer record should be pooled for batch file generation of RBI	Customer account is debited but record not reflected in batch file	fail	Critical
TC_004	USCA-013	Fund Transfer	Generation of fund transfer batch file for RBI	1. Login as CBS user 2. Select Reports - RBI batch file generation 3. Select transfer type as RTGS, NEFT etc. 3. Generate Batch File for RBI	Batch file for RBI should be generated and saved in predetermined location	Batch file is generated	pass	-
TC_005	USCA-013	Fund Transfer	Generation of fund transfer batch file for RBI- Record wise check	Verify the Batch file with the business rules.	All records since last batch report and as per time slot should be available	All records are not reflected	fail	Critical
TC_006	USCA-014	Fund Transfer	Upload of fund transfer response file from RBI	1. Login as CBS User 2. Select Batch Update 3. Upload response file from RBI to CBS	File is successfully uploaded	File is successfully uploaded	pass	-
TC_007	USCA-014	Fund Transfer	Upload of fund transfer response file from RBI- Check accounts update	1. Login as CBS User 2. Select Batch Update 3. Upload response file from RBI to CBS 4. Verify whether respective accounts are updated	All records should be updated as per RBI response file	All records are updated as per RBI response file	pass	-

9 Reference Diagrams

Define Reference Diagrams: GAP Analysis (question 36)

GAP Analysis					
Functionalities or New capabilities	As-Is	To-Be	Gap	Priority	Comments
Operating Model	Current Operating Model	Future Operating Model	Future Capabilities	Medium	Need to achieve the future operating model to keep the pace with future requirements.
Technology	System is in VB 6.0	System to be build in .NET	Technology up gradation	High	Need latest technology to deal with system
Legal / Compliances	Nil	As per the new regulation, the account department needs to implement Sarbane-Oxlay audit process	Incorporate new process or update existing process to implement the accounting regulation	High	Implementation is mandatory requirement.
Industry Standards	Many Competitors have started providing online shopping facilities to the busy customers	Need to provide online shopping facilities in addition to store business	Online shopping system that provide real-time shopping experience.	High	It is important to retain existing customers, add new ones for the growth of future business.
Performance	Old system is unable process more than 50 request in a minutes	Future anticipated request will be the ability of system to handle 500 request in a minutes	Require 10 times faster system		With current and projected growth, the system must cater to be updated to cater to existing and future needs.
Look and Feel	Outdated site in terms of look and feel, navigations, menus and pictures i.e. outdated website	Need attractive site with updated content, great graphics, navigations and user friendly experience	Updated and user friendly website with advanced features.	Medium	Younger customers are techno-savvy and their expectations are more than what existing system can offer.

Requirement Catalogue (Requirement catalogue question 133

GLOBAL BANK LTD

ONLINE BANKING SOLUTION

REQUIREMENT CATALOGUE for Online Banking Solution)

Service description	Linked Business Outcomes	Consumer	REQUIREMENT ID	REQUIREMENT USE CASE	BRIEF DESCRIPTION	CRITICALITY (MOSCOW)	CATEGORY (BUSINESS/REGULATORY)	TYPE (FUNCTIONAL/NON FUNCTIONAL)	BENEFIT (1-5)	COST (EFFORTS 5)	VALUE INDEX (B/C)	APPROVED	STATUS
To provide online facility to bank customers to carry out different types of banking transactions without the need to physically visit the branches	Increased productivity, reduction in transaction cost, increased market penetration	Consumer using worldwide Internet Services	FR-001	USCA-001	User Registration is mandatory	M	BUSINESS	FUNCTIONAL	5	3	1.67	YES	TESTING
To provide online facility to bank customers to carry out different types of banking transactions without the need to physically visit the branches	Increased productivity, reduction in transaction cost, increased market penetration	Consumer using worldwide Internet Services	FR-002	USCA-008	Change Password	M	BUSINESS	FUNCTIONAL	4	3	1.33	YES	TESTING
To provide online facility to bank customers to carry out different types of banking transactions without the need to physically visit the branches	Increased productivity, reduction in transaction cost, increased market penetration	Consumer using worldwide Internet Services	FR-003	USCA-009	Reset Password	M	BUSINESS	FUNCTIONAL	3	3	1.00	YES	TESTING
To provide online facility to bank customers to carry out different types of banking transactions without the need to physically visit the branches	Increased productivity, reduction in transaction cost, increased market penetration	Consumer using worldwide Internet Services	FR-004	USCA-010	Access to Transaction Statement	M	BUSINESS	FUNCTIONAL	4	4	1.00	YES	DEVELOPMENT
To provide online facility to bank customers to carry out different types of banking transactions without the need to physically visit the branches	Increased productivity, reduction in transaction cost, increased market penetration	Consumer using worldwide Internet Services	FR-005	USCA-012	Fund Transfer-Inter Bank	M	BUSINESS	FUNCTIONAL	4	4	1.00	YES	TESTING
To provide online facility to bank customers to carry out different types of banking transactions without the need to physically visit the branches	Increased productivity, reduction in transaction cost, increased market penetration	Consumer using worldwide Internet Services	FR-006	USCA-012	Fund Transfer-Intra Bank	M	BUSINESS	FUNCTIONAL	5	4	1.25	YES	TESTING
To provide online facility to bank customers to carry out different types of banking transactions without the need to physically visit the branches	Increased productivity, reduction in transaction cost, increased market penetration	Consumer using worldwide Internet Services	FR-007	USCA-011	Registration of beneficiary account	M	BUSINESS	FUNCTIONAL	5	4	1.25	YES	TESTING
To provide online facility to bank customers to carry out different types of banking transactions without the need to physically visit the branches	Increased productivity, reduction in transaction cost, increased market penetration	Consumer using worldwide Internet Services	FR-008	USCA-013	Generation of fund transfer file for RBI	M	REGULATORY	FUNCTIONAL	4	3	1.33	YES	DEVELOPMENT
To provide online facility to bank customers to carry out different types of banking transactions without the need to physically visit the branches	Increased productivity, reduction in transaction cost, increased market penetration	Consumer using worldwide Internet Services	FR-009	USCA-014	Upload of response file from RBI	M	REGULATORY	FUNCTIONAL	4	3	1.33	YES	DEVELOPMENT
To provide online facility to bank customers to carry out different types of banking transactions without the need to physically visit the branches	Increased productivity, reduction in transaction cost, increased market penetration	Consumer using worldwide Internet Services	FR-010		Email and SMS alert to customers	S	BUSINESS	FUNCTIONAL	3	2	1.50	YES	REQUIREMENTS

10 Reference

- A Guide to the Business Analysis Body of Knowledge® (BABOK® Guide) Version 2.0. By International Institute of Business Analysis (IIBA), Canada 2009.

- A Guide to the Business Analysis Body of Knowledge® (BABOK® Guide) Version 3.0. By International Institute of Business Analysis (IIBA), Canada 2015

- [Amsterdam, 2013] Total Solution Event System by z Amsterdam. IBM ftp://www.redbooks.ibm.com/redbooks/2013_ITSO_Total_Solution_Event_System_z_Amsterdam/track_6_Keeping_your_Applications_fit_for_the_Future/TSE_AMS_AD09_Application_Decommissioning.pdf accessed on Feb 12th, 2017.

- [Baxter, Ian Sommerville , 2011] Socio-technical systems: From design methods to systems engineering Gordon Baxter, Ian Sommerville. Interacting with Computers, Volume 23, Issue 1, 1 January 2011, Pages 4–17,

- [Beedle, Sutherland et el, 2002] Agile: Software Development with Scrumby Ken Schwaber, Mike Beedle, Jeff Sutherland and others, Prentice Hall, 2002)

- [Berczuk and Appleton, 2004] Software Configuration Management Patterns: Effective Teamwork, Practical ...By Stephen P. Berczuk, Brad Appleton. Addison-Wesley Professional, July 2004)

- [Bohm, 2009] The SWOT Analysis: A Seminar Paper by Anja Bohm, GRIN Verlag, 2009, p.i

- [Bolles, 2002] Building Project-Management Centers of Excellence By Dennis Bolles. AMACOM, a division of American Management Association, in 2002 page 135-136

- [Calero and Piattini, 2015] Green in Software Engineering by Corol Calero, Mario Piattini, Editors. Springer 2015 pp. 68-70

- Centers for Medicare & Medicaid Services (CMS) Office of Information Service (2008). Selecting a development approach. Web article. United States Department of Health and Human Services (HHS). Accessed on 21 Nov 20162.

- Carkenord, 2014]Three proven ways business analysts help prevent scope creep by By Carkenord, Barbara A. 2014 (https://www.pmi.org/learning/library/business-analysts-help-prevent-scope-creep-9352)

- [Castella, 2014] Castilla, Dalila, "A Hybrid Approach Using RUP and Scrum as a Software Development Strategy" (2014). UNF Theses and Dissertations. Paper 514. http://digitalcommons.unf.edu/etd/514

- [Chemuturi, M. 2013]. Requirements Engineering and Management for Software Development Projects. Requirements Engineering and

Management for Software Development Projects by Chemuturi, Murali. Springer. 2013

- [Cho, 2009]. A Hybrid Software Development Method For Large-scale Projects: Rational Unified Process With Scrum By Juyun Cho. Issues in Information System in Volume X, No. 2, 2009

- [Cockburn, 2000] Writing Effective Use Cases by Alitstair Cockburn's Addison-Wesley Professional, 6 Oct 2000

- [Codling, 1992] Best Practice Benchmarking: A Management Guide By Sylvia Codling. Gower Publishing, 1992 Ltd.page 7-9

- [Davis, 1993] Software Requirements: Objects, Functions and States, by A.M. Davis. Englewood Cliffs, 1993

- [Freeman, 2010] Strategic Management: A Stakeholder Approach by R. Edward Freeman. Cambridge University Press, 11 Mar 2010]

- [Frankel, 1986] Guidance on Software Package Selection By Sheila Frankel, United States. National Bureau of Standards, in 1986, page 61-72)

- [Griffin, 2007] Fundamentals of Management by Ricky Griffin Cengage Learning, 11 Oct 2007 page 74-75

- [Ian Graham, 2008]. Requirements Modelling and Specification for Service Oriented Architecture by Ian Gram. Ohn Wiley & Sons, Nov 2008, page 177.
- [Harel, 1987] A Visual Formalism for Complex Systems. Science of Computing Programming, Vol 8, NO 3, 1987 by D. Harel: Statecharts – pages 231-274

- [Hass, 2003] Configuration Management Principles and Practice By Anne Mette Jonassen Hass. Addison-Wesley Professional in 2003, page 3)

- [Hartel, 1987] A Visual Formalism for Complex Systems. Science of Computing Programming, Vol 8, NO 3, 1987 by D. Harel: Statecharts pages 231-274

- [Hollander, 2000] A Guide to Software Package Evaluation & Selection: The R2ISC Method, by Nathan Hollander, Volume 1 by AMACOM, 2000)

- Jacobson Ivar, Christerson Magnus, Jonsson Patrik, Övergaard Gunnar, Object-Oriented Software Engineering - A Use Case Driven Approach, Addison-Wesley, 1992.

- Jacobson, Ivar; Spence, Ian; Bittner, Kurt (December 2011). "Use Case 2.0: The Guide to Succeeding with Use Cases". Ivar Jacobson International. Retrieved 2014-05-05.

- [Jane, 2014] Gap Analysis by Sandhya Jane. Blogpost https://businessanalysis-anisan.blogspot.hk/2014/09/gap-analysis.html) accessed on Mar 14th, 2017.

- [Jane, 2016] Career Paths for Business Analysts . Blogpost. Bloglink: (https://businessanalysis-anisan.blogspot.hk/2016/03/career-paths-for-business-analyst.html) accessed on Aug 26th, 2017

- [Jane, 2016] Business Need Blog by Sandhya Jane. Blogpost. (https://businessanalysis-anisan.blogspot.hk/2016/04/business-analysis-business-need.html) accessed on Nov 2nd, 2016

- [Jane, 2016] How to Conduct Stakeholder Analysis by Sandhya Jane. Blogpost. 2016. (https://businessanalysisguru.wordpress.com/2016/12/18/how-to-conduct-stakeholder-analysis/) accessed on Jan 30th, 2006

- [Jane, 2016] What Business analyst must know about Agile Approach? by Sandhya Jane. Blog Post. 2016. (https://businessanalysis-anisan.blogspot.com/2016/04/business-analyst-must-know-agile-scrum.html) accessed on Jan 15th, 2017

- [Johnson, Scholes et el, 2008] Exploring Corporate Strategy, 8th Edition by Johnson, G., Scholes, K and Whittington, R (2008). FT Prentice Hall, Harlow.

- [Kaliszewski , 2012] Quantitative Pareto Analysis by Cone Separation Technique Ignacy Kaliszewski Springer Science & Business Media, 6 Dec 2012[

- Kanaracus, 2009] SAP project costs cited in jeweler's bankruptcy filing By Chris Kanaracus. Comptuer World. 2009. (http://www.computerworld.com/article/2530405/it-careers/sap-project-costs-cited-in-jeweler-s-bankruptcy-filing.html). Jan 14th, 2009 accessed on Mar 12th, 2017

- [Katuscáková and Jasecková, 2016] The Share of Knowledge Management Subjects Within Study Programmes in the Library and Information Sciences. Katuscáková, Marcela, and Galina Jasecková. European Conference on Knowledge Management, Academic Conferences International Limited, Sept. 2016, p. 420.

- [Kossak, Illibauer et el, 2015] A Rigorous Semantics for BPMN 2.0 Process Diagrams By Felix Kossak, Christa Illibauer, Verena Geist, Jan Kubovy, Christine Natschläger, Thomas Ziebermayr, Theodorich Kopetzky, Bernhard Freudenthaler, Klaus-Dieter Schewe by Springer published in 2015. page 30

- [Kotonya,Sommenville, 1998] Requirements Engineering: Processes and Techniques by Chichester Kotonya, G. and Sommerville, I.., UK: John Wiley and Sons. 1998

- [Marakas, O'Brien , 2010] Management information systems (10th ed.) by Marakas James A. O'Brien, George M. McGraw-Hill/Irwin. New York 201. pp. 485–489.

- [Marr, 2015] The Difference Between Big Data and a Lot of Data by Bernard Marr an article published on data-informed.com in 2015 http://data-informed.com/the-difference-between-big-data-and-a-lot-of-data/

- [McConnell, 2001] Rapid development. Taming wild software schedules by Steve McConnell. 14th ed. Microsoft Press, Redmond 2001 ISBN 1-556-15900-5

- [Needle, 2010] Business in Context: An Introduction to Business and Its Environment By David Needle. South Western Educational Publishing; 5th Revised edition (March 1, 2010) page 4 and 5

- [Nielsen and Molich, 1990] Heuristic evaluation of user interfaces by Nielsen, J., & Molich, R. (1990). Proceedings from ACM CHI'90 Conference. Seattle, WA, 249-256.
- [Nielsen, 1994] Usability Engineering by Nielsen, J. (1994). Academic Press San Diego:.

- [NIELSEN , 1995] Usability Heuristics for User Interface Design by JAKOB NIELSEN on January 1, 1995

- [Pahl, Richter, 2009] Swot Analysis - Idea, Methodology and a Practical Approach by Nadine Pahl, Anne Richter. GRIN Verlag, 2009

- [Paul, Cadle, 2011] Business Analysis, by Debra Paul, (Editors) Donald Yeats and James Cadle, Second edition, BCS, UK 2011.

- [Pohl and Rupp, 2011] Requirement Engineering Fundamentals by Klaus Pohl and Chris Rupp, Published by Rockynook, 2011, p.34

- [Pohl and Rupp, 2011] Requirement Engineering Fundamentals by Kalus Pohl, Chris Rupp,. Rockynook, 2011. Page 134

- [Porter, 1980] Competitive Strategy: Techniques for Analysing Industries and Competitors, by porter, M (1980) Free Press, New York

- [Porter, 2008] Competitive Strategy: Techniques for Analyzing Industries and Competitors by Michael. E. Porter Simon and Schuster, 30 Jun 2008

- [Rational Software White Paper, 1998] Rational Unified Process: Best Practices for Software Development Teams by Rational Software White Paper TP026B, Rev 11/01)

- [Rocha, Ana Maria Correia, 2014] New Perspectives in Information Systems and Technologies, Volume 2 edited by Álvaro Rocha, Ana Maria Correia, Felix . B Tan, Karl . A Stroetmann. Springer in 2014, page 95-96

- [Rocha, Correia et el, 2014] New Perspectives in Information Systems and Technologies, Volume 2 edited by Álvaro Rocha, Ana Maria Correia, Felix . B Tan, Karl . A Stroetmann published by Springer in 2014, page 95-96

- [Rowel and Alfeche, 1997] Requirements Engineering A good practice guide by Ramos Rowel and Kurts Alfeche, John Wiley and Sons. 1997

- [Sabri, Gupta et el., 2006] Purchase Order Management Best Practices: Process,
  Technology, and Change Management by Ehap H. Sabri, Arun P. Gupta, Michael A. Beitle. J. . Ross Publishing, 15 Nov 2006 Page 197-198

- [Sarsby, 2016] A Guide to SWOT for Business Studies Students by Allen Sarsby, Lulu.com 2016 p.18

- [Schneider and Winters, 1998]. Applying Use Cases: A Practical Guide. Schneider, G. and J. P. Winters (1998) Reading, Mass., Addison Wesley.

- [Schreiner, 2007] The Bridge and Beyond: Business Analysis Extends its Role and Reach by Schreiner, K., Published by IEEE Published in: IT Professional (Volume 9, Issue: 6) in 2007

- [Sommerville, 2003] Academic notes by Ian Sommerville, Link: (http://www.inf.ed.ac.uk/teaching/courses/ip/CS2Ah0405-SoftwareRequirements.pdf) accessed on Aug 30th, 2017.

- [Sorrentino , 2016] (Configuration Management: Implementation, Principles, and Applications for ... By Joseph Sorrentino published by CRC in 2016, page Xiii)

- [Sorrentino, 2016] Configuration Management: Implementation, Principles, and Applications for ... By Joseph Sorrentino. CRC in 2016, page Xiii

- [Stamatis, 2003] Failure Mode and Effect Analysis: FMEA from Theory to Execution D. H. Stamatis ASQ Quality Press, 2003

- [Stellman, Greene, 2005] Stellman, Andrew; Greene, Jennifer (2005). Applied Software Project Management. O'Reilly Media

- [Świątek, Borzemski, et el, 2015] International Conference on Information Systems Architecture and Technology – ISAT 2015 –, Part 3 by Jerzy Świątek, Leszek Borzemski, Adam Grzech, Zofia Wilimowska Springer, 23 Feb 2016 Information Systems Architecture and Technology: Proceedings of 36th

- Systems Engineering Fundamentals Defense Acquisition University Press, 2001

- [UML 2.5, 2009] UML by OMG Unified Modeling Language TM (OMG UML) pages 389-427 OMG Unified Modelling Language TM (OMG UML) Version 2.5

- [WALKER, Adrian; et al. 1990]Knowledge Systems and Prolog by WALKER, Adrian; et al. (1990). Addison-Wesley. ISBN 0-201-52424-4.)

- [Walton, 1997]Handbook of Counselling in Organizations, Volume 1 Michael Carroll, Michael Walton SAGE, 28 Feb 1997, page 102

- [Windle and Abreo , 2003] Software Requirements Using the Unified Process: A Practical Approach by Daniel R. Windle, L. Rene Abreo, Prentice Hall Professional 2003, pp.58-59

- http://www.cisco.com/c/en/us/products/collateral/services/high-availability/white_paper_c11-458050.html accessed on Jan 12th, 2017

- A Thesis Submitted to the Department of Computer Science and Engineering of BRAC University by Md. Jahangir Hossain and A.T.M.Mahmudul Hasan

(http://dspace.bracu.ac.bd/bitstream/handle/10361/462/Online%20he alth%20information%20system%20BD%20doctor.pdf)

- Source: https://explorable.com/surveys-and-questionnaires and http://onlinelibrary.wiley.com/doi/10.1111/ina.12400/full accessed on Mar 13th, 2017

- https://www.justice.gov/archive/jmd/irm/lifecycle/ch1.htm accessed on Aug 29th, 2017.

- Scrum Institute Website (http://www.scrum-institute.org/What_Is_Scrum.php Accessed on April 19, 16)

- University of New York. (https://www.nyu.edu/content/dam/nyu/prgmServices/documents/Project%20Closeout%20Template.doc)

- System Decommission, by Department of General Services (DGS) (http://www.bestpractices.osi.ca.gov/system_development/system_decommission.shtml) accessed on Apr 12th, 2017

- Business Need Statement Template (https://www2.cdc.gov/cdcup/library/templates/CDC_UP_Business_Needs_Statement_Template.doc)

- Vision and Scope Document Template (http://www.wsdot.wa.gov/eesc/bridge/software/Files/vision_and_scope.doc) accessed on June 2016

11 Aknowledgement

This is my third literary work after the process of writing my debut novel, *Second Spring*.

The thought of first writing this book occurred to me while I was answering a question on Quora (www.quora.com), a leading question and answer website. Thereafter, I started putting my thoughts together to write a 'question and answer book' on business analysis to offer a well-researched compendium on the most commonly asked questions in the subject. The answers are aimed at providing a holistic insight into the varied aspect of business analysis and scope to channelize the thoughts.

I wish to express my sincerest gratitude to all my mentees for both freely exchanging their thoughts and immensely inspiring me in finishing the work.

I also would like to give credit to my both editors, Manish and Beth, who have painstakingly reviewed the manuscript several times.
I sincerely hope that the readers will find this latest book of mine as well as my future projects eminently useful.

Sandhya Jane

Made in the USA
Monee, IL
28 April 2026

49136504R00187